Dostoevsky's
The Brothers Karamazov

Dostoevsky's *The Brothers Karamazov*

JULIAN W. CONNOLLY

B L O O M S B U R Y
LONDON • NEW DELHI • NEW YORK • SYDNEY

Bloomsbury Academic
An imprint of Bloomsbury Publishing Plc

175 Fifth Avenue	50 Bedford Square
New York	London
NY 10010	WC1B 3DP
USA	UK

www.bloomsbury.com

First published 2013

Library of Congress Cataloging-in-Publication Data
Connolly, Julian W.
Dostoevsky's The Brothers Karamazov / by Julian W. Connolly.
pages ; cm
Includes bibliographical references and index.
ISBN 978-1-4411-0847-0 (hardback : alkaline paper)–
ISBN 978-1-4411-3531-5 (paperback : alkaline paper)
1. Dostoyevsky, Fyodor, 1821-1881. Brat'ia Karamazovy. I. Title.
PG3325.B73C66 2013
891.73'3–dc23
2012031988

ISBN: HB: 978-1-4411-0847-0
PB: 978-1-4411-3531-5

Typeset by Fakenham Prepress Solutions, Fakenham, Norfolk NR21 8NN
Printed and bound in the United States of America

CONTENTS

A NOTE ON TRANSLITERATION

Spelling of Russian names follows the Library of Congress system without diacritics, with some modifications. Commonly adopted spellings (e.g. Tolstoy, Fyodor, Smerdyakov) are used, and names ending in –yi, -ii are spelled "y" (e.g. Dmitry)

Titles in Russian (and bibliographical material) are not modified in this way.

Main texts used

Quotations from *The Brothers Karamazov* are taken from the translation by Constance Garnett and revised by Ralph E. Matlaw and Susan McReynolds Oddo (New York: W. W. Norton, 2011). Some translations have been adjusted for accuracy or consistency.

References to the Russian edition of Dostoevsky's work are to the thirty-volume *Polnoe sobranie sochinenii* (Leningrad: Nauka, 1972–90). These references will be identified with a parenthetical note containing the abbreviation *PSS* and the volume and page number.

Dates

All dates relating to Dostoevsky's life are based on the Old Style calendar in use in Russia at the time.

CHAPTER ONE

Contexts

Dostoevsky's life

Fyodor Mikhailovich Dostoevsky was born on 30 October [Old Style] 1821 in Moscow, Russia. He was the second son of a retired military doctor, Mikhail Andreevich Dostoevsky, who had an appointment and an apartment at the Mariinsky Hospital for the Poor in an impoverished district of the city. The doctor was a proud and exacting individual subject to pronounced moments of depression and irritability. Dostoevsky's mother, Maria Fyodorovna (née Nechaeva), in contrast, was a warm and loving woman who taught Fyodor to read and instilled in him a religious spark that remained with him for the rest of his life. She would take her elder children (she had eight in all) on annual visits to the Trinity-St. Sergius Monastery, about 50 miles northeast of Moscow. Due to his diligent service to the State, Mikhail Dostoevsky earned the right to enter the ranks of the Russian nobility, and in 1828 he registered himself and his two sons, Mikhail and Fyodor, in the rolls of the nobility in Moscow. Three years later, he acquired a small estate called Darovoe, and it was here that young Fyodor spent some of his happiest summer months as a child. In 1833, he and his older brother Mikhail began attending a day school in Moscow, and a year later they moved on to Chermak's boarding school, one of the best in Moscow. They would spend the work week at the school and return home on the weekends. Dostoevsky would later depict the contrast he experienced between the rigors of school and the warmth of the home in his first novel, *Poor Folk* (*Bednye liudi*, 1846).

Dostoevsky's life changed dramatically at the end of the 1830s. His beloved mother died in February 1837, and later that year Fyodor and Mikhail would be taken by their father to St. Petersburg to prepare for entrance into the Academy of Military Engineers, thus undertaking a career path for which Fyodor had little enthusiasm. The two young men entered the Academy in 1838, and although Fyodor took all the required engineering classes, his real interests lay in the realm of literature. He became swept up in the contemporary enthusiasm for literary Romanticism, particularly German Romanticism, including the works of E. T. A. Hoffman, Johann Wolfgang von Goethe, and Friedrich Schiller. A voracious reader, he engaged in heated exchanges about literature with a few close friends, and he became editor of the student newspaper.

While Dostoevsky was at the Academy, he received shocking news from home: his father was found dead in June 1839 under very mysterious circumstances. Although the official cause of death was reported to be a stroke, rumor had it that Mikhail Andreevich had been murdered by peasants outraged at abuses he had committed on his estate, to which he had retreated after the death of his wife. Although there is scant evidence of Dostoevsky's personal feelings about the event, a likely consequence was a heightened sensitivity to the issue of class injustice in the Russian countryside, where a large percentage of the populace were serfs under the dominion of their gentry landowners.

In 1841, Dostoevsky was promoted to the rank of field ensign-engineer, and he now could live outside the Academy while taking continuing to take classes there. His graduation from the Academy followed in 1843 and he was assigned to a drafting position in the St. Petersburg Engineering Command. He plugged away at this job for a year, and finally resigned his position in 1844, with the official discharge coming in October. Dostoevsky was now free to devote himself to his real passion—literary creativity. Although he had earlier tried his hand at historical dramas (*Mary Stuart* and *Boris Godunov*, neither of which has survived), Dostoevsky's first published work was a translation of Honoré de Balzac's *Eugénie Grandet* (1844). He also began working on what would become his first novel, *Poor Folk*. This short novel in letters, which chronicles the travails of an elderly clerk and a young woman

living in severely straitened circumstances, achieved immediate
success among the important literati of the day, including the critic
Vissarion Belinksy. Dostoevsky was elated by the praise showered
upon him, only to have his ego crushed with the appearance of his
second novel, The Double (Dvoinik), which features an undistin-
guished bureaucrat who believes that his position at work and in
society is being taken over by a conniving double. Critics panned
the work, seeing it as little more than an imitation of stories by the
celebrated Russian writer Nikolay Gogol. Discouraged, Dostoevsky
published only one work in 1847, a story of obsession entitled
"The Landlady" ("Khoziaika"). In 1848, however, Dostoevsky's
productivity increased, and that year saw the publication of several
short stories, including "A Weak Heart" ("Slaboe serdtse"), and
the lyrical "White Nights" ("Belye nochi").
    While working on his these texts Dostoevsky also took part in
social groups devoted to the discussion of current events in politics
and society as well as literature. One group that met in the home
of Mikhail Petrashevsky debated prospects for reform in Russian
society, but Dostoevsky became drawn to a smaller group with
more radical aims. This group, which met at the apartment of
Alexander Palm and Sergei Durov, debated prospects for publishing
subversive propaganda on an illegal printing press. These plans
never came to fruition, however, for in the wake of government
uneasiness over the spread of revolutionary unrest in Europe in
1848, Dostoevsky was awakened in his apartment on the morning
of 23 April 1849 and put under arrest for his association with the
Petrashevsky circle. He was incarcerated in the Peter-Paul Fortress
in St. Petersburg while the authorities investigated the group. A
new novel by Dostoevsky, Netochka Nezvanova, which featured
a young woman as the first-person narrator and protagonist, had
begun appearing in a journal in 1849, but it was interrupted by
Dostoevsky's arrest, and he only managed to complete one short
story, "A Little Hero" ("Malenkii geroi," published 1857) during
his imprisonment.
    When the investigators finished their work, the court recom-
mended the death sentence for Dostoevsky and his fellow
"conspirators," but this sentence was commuted by Tsar Nicholas I
to a lesser punishment: four years of penal servitude to be followed
by an indefinite term of service in the Russian army. In an act of
stunning cruelty, the prisoners were not immediately told of their

true sentences. On the contrary, they were led out to an execution site set up in Semenovsky Square, where their death sentences were read out to them. It was only then that an official came riding up on a horse to tell them of their true fate. Understandably, this experience affected Dostoevsky deeply, and it would play a role in his later fiction. That very day—22 December 1849—Dostoevsky wrote to his brother about his renewed appreciation for life: "Life is a gift, life is happiness, each minute could have been an eternity of happiness […] I swear to you I won't lose hope and will preserve my heart and spirit in purity. I'll be reborn for the better" (*Complete Letters* 1: 181).

Dostoevsky would spend four years in a prison labor camp in Omsk, Siberia, and during that entire time he was allowed no correspondence or reading material other than an edition of the New Testament given to him on the way to the camp. Released in January 1854, he later summarized the experience in a letter to his brother Andrey: "And those four years I consider a time during which I was buried alive and locked up in a coffin. I can't even tell you, my friend, what a horrible time that was. It was inexpressible, unending suffering, because every hour, every minute weighed on my soul like a stone" (6 November 1854; *Complete Letters* 1: 201). Dostoevsky was more expansive about the difficulties of his internment in a letter he wrote to his brother Mikhail in February 1854, but the most comprehensive account is a fictionalized memoir entitled *Notes from the Dead House* (*Zapiski iz mertvogo doma*), published over ten years later (1860–62). There Dostoevsky not only provides vivid descriptions of the camp's inhabitants, both good and evil, he also discloses the dreadful distortions of human conduct that arise when people are deprived of freedom.

Once out of prison, Dostoevsky served as a private in a battalion in Semipalatinsk. There he met his future wife, Maria Dmitrievna Isaeva. Isaeva was married, but her husband died in August 1855, and Dostoevsky began to woo the widow. In the autumn of 1855 Dostoevsky was promoted to the rank of non-commissioned officer, and he subsequently received a promotion to the rank of ensign on 1 October 1856. Early the next year, on 6 February 1857, he married Maria Dmitrievna. In January 1858, Dostoevsky begins seeking permission to be allowed to retire from the army and return to Western Russia. In March he received that permission, and he finally returned to St. Petersburg in December 1959, exactly ten years after he had left it. He had already resumed his literary activity during this time, and 1859 saw the publication of two satirical works, "Uncle's Dream" ("Diadushkin son") and "The Village of Stepanchikovo and Its Inhabitants" ("Selo Stepanchikovo i ego obitateli"). Back in St. Petersburg, Dostoevsky joined his brother Mikhail in starting a journal, *Time* (*Vremia*), which became the publishing outlet for a new novel, *The Humiliated and the Insulted* (*Unizhennye i oskorblennye*, 1861), which depicts the pathetic vulnerability of the weak before the predations of the strong.

In 1862, Dostoevsky took his first trip to Western Europe, and he recorded his reactions in a short book entitled *Winter Notes on Summer Impressions* (*Zimnie zametki o letnikh vpechatleniiakh*, 1863). Here Dostoevsky excoriates the bourgeois smugness of the French, and depicts in vivid hues the capitalist hell he found in London. Europe, he realized, had become corrupt and venal and it had nothing more to offer Russia. In Russia itself, however, the political climate was anything but calm. The authorities closed down Dostoevsky's journal *Time* in May 1863, because it had not supported with sufficient vigor the regime's efforts to suppress the ongoing Polish independence movement. Dostoevsky had become involved in a love affair with a young woman named Apollinaria Suslova, and he made plans to travel to Italy with her in the summer of 1863. Preoccupied with financial concerns and the *Time* problem, Dostoevsky delayed his departure, and Suslova went on to Paris without him. Finally, Dostoevsky left St. Petersburg to join her, but lured by the fantasy of winning a fortune, stopped at a gambling spa on the way. When he arrived in Paris, he found that she had fallen in love with someone else, but he persuaded her to travel with him to Italy nonetheless. The trip was full of emotional turmoil, and Dostoevsky would transmute these intense personal experiences (tortured love, obsession with gambling) into his short novel *The Gambler* (*Igrok*, 1866).

Russia in the 1860s was awash with political debate. From Dostoevsky's perspective, the leading progressives of the day were disturbingly under the sway of Western materialism and atheistic socialism, and he sought to meet this challenge both in his creative fiction and in his publicistic journalism. In *Notes from the Underground* (*Zapiski iz podpol'ia*, 1864) he champions the importance of individual free will in the face of deterministic schemes purporting to ensure human happiness. At the same time, through his depiction of the narrator, Dostoevsky reveals the corrosive consequences of a fear of intimacy, the refusal to allow oneself to be loved by (and to love) another person. Dostoevsky took up these issues again in one of his most famous novels, *Crime and Punishment* (*Prestuplenie i nakazanie*, 1866), but in that work, his isolated hero Rodion Raskolnikov finds a path to redemption and salvation through the devotion of the selfless prostitute Sonya Marmeladov. Dead in spirit, the murderer Raskolnikov is resurrected by Sonya's unconditional love.

Dostoevsky's wife Maria died in 1864, and she was shortly followed in death by Dostoevsky's beloved brother Mikhail. Increasingly burdened by debt in the mid-1860s, Dostoevsky signed a contract with a publisher named Stellovsky that required the submission of a new novel to Stellovsky by November 1, 1866; otherwise Dostoevsky would surrender the rights to all his future works without compensation for nine years. Frantic as the deadline approached, Dostoevsky hired a stenographer named Anna Grigorievna Snitkina, to whom he dictated *The Gambler* in just under a month's time. Having met the terms of the contract, Dostoevsky asked the young woman to marry him, and she agreed. They got married on February 15, 1867, and she would bring a palpable measure of stability to the writer's emotional and financial affairs.

Dostoevsky and his wife left Russia for Western Europe in April 1867, and they remained there for the next four years. While in Geneva, Anna gave birth to a baby girl named Sofia, but the great joy that the child brought the couple was cut short by the infant's sudden death in May 1868. Dostoevsky's immense grief is evident in a letter he wrote shortly after the event: "And now people tell me by way of consolation that I'll have more children. But where is Sonya? Where is that little person for whom I state boldly that I would accept crucifixion if only she could be alive?" (18 May 1868; *Complete Letters* 3: 76). Dostoevsky's shock at the untimely loss of his beloved daughter would inform Ivan Karamazov's agonized reflections on the injustice of the suffering of children in *The Brothers Karamazov*, as well as his depictions of grief over the death of children in that novel. In time, Dostoevsky and his wife did have other children, including a daughter Lyubov, born in September 1869.

During this period, Dostoevsky worked on a new novel, (*The Idiot*, 1868), in which he hoped to depict a "perfectly beautiful human person" ("polozhitel'no prekrasnogo cheloveka" [Jan 1, 1868; *Complete Letters* 3: 17]). At the center of the novel stands Prince Lev Myshkin, an extraordinarily empathetic man who seems to draw out the latent conflicts and tensions within the people around him. Although his intentions are positive, he is unable to check the destructive passions unleashed in others, and the murder of the proud Nastasya Filippovna by the merchant Rogozhin plunges Myshkin into insanity. Dostoevsky also contemplated large novels dealing with the central issues of faith, sin, and the potential for regeneration. One project was entitled *Atheism* (*Ateizm*) while the other was a five-novel opus called *The Life of a Great Sinner* (*Zhitie velikogo greshnika*). Of the latter Dostoevsky wrote: "The main question, which is pursued in all the parts, is the same one that I have been tormented by consciously and unconsciously my whole life—the existence of God" (25 March 1870; *Complete Letters* 3: 248). Dostoevsky never completed these projects, however, for his attention was diverted by the murder of a Russian student in Moscow by a small group of political radicals in November 1869. Dostoevsky set out to write a "pamphlet novel" castigating these radicals, and he incorporated some elements of the undeveloped projects into this new work. The end product, a novel entitled *The Devils* (*Besy*, 1871–72), features a pair of characters who have a baleful impact on the society through which they move: the charismatic Stavrogin, who is haunted by a crime he committed against a child and seeks in vain for a way to assuage his guilt, and the demonic Pyotr Verkhovensky, who sews confusion and destruction among the gullible people taken in by his lies and deceptions.

In July 1871 the Dostoevsky family returned to Russia, and their first son, Fyodor, was born on July 16. Over the next few years, Dostoevsky continued his journalistic activity, most notably a series of columns entitled *A Writer's Diary* (*Dnevnik pisatelia*), which eventually became an independent publication with an impressive number of individual subscribers. Dostoevsky used this outlet to publish his views in several genres, from sharply worded polemical essays to distinctive short stories, including "A Gentle Creature" ("Krotkaia,"1876) and "The Dream of a Ridiculous Man" ("Son smeshnogo cheloveka," 1877). He also published a

novel called *The Adolescent* (*Podrostok*, 1875), but this representation of fractured family relations did not meet with widespread
success. Dostoevsky eventually channeled his creative powers
into the novel that would cap his illustrious career, *The Brothers
Karamazov* (*Brat'ia Karamazovy*, 1879–80). During the writing of
the novel, Dostoevsky's youngest son, Alexey, died at the age of
three, and this terrible loss underlies Dostoevsky's treatment of the
death of children in his great novel. The publication of the novel in
periodical installments was greeted by the reading public with deep
interest and acclaim, and Dostoevsky's reputation as a figure who
had important truths to communicate to the people was further
bolstered by a speech he delivered at the celebrations marking
the unveiling of a monument to Alexander Pushkin in Moscow
in 1880. At the very height of his fame and prestige, however,
Dostoevsky, who suffered from emphysema, began coughing up
blood, and he passed away on 28 January 1881. His grave lies in
the cemetery of the Alexander Nevsky Monastery in St. Petersburg.

Dostoevsky and the struggle between faith and doubt

In his *Writer's Diary* Dostoevsky wrote in 1873: "I came from a
family that was Russian and pious [...] In our family we knew
the Gospels virtually from our earliest childhood" (*Writer's Diary*
1: 289). Both of Dostoevsky's parents were deeply religious, and
according to his brother Andrey, he and his siblings were taught to
read from a Russian translation of a German religious text entitled
*One Hundred and Four Sacred Stories from the Old and New
Testaments*,[1] just as Father Zosima would later relate that he had
done in *The Brothers Karamazov* (Book 6, Chapter 2). Dostoevsky
retained his deep respect for religious texts and Russian spirituality
throughout his life, although he was intimately familiar with the
assaults on religion carried out by waves of progressive thinkers
throughout the mid-nineteenth century. Nor was he immune to
the arguments of these thinkers. As he wrote in a letter to Natalia
Fonvizina soon after his release from prison camp in 1854: "I'll
tell you of myself that I have been a child of the age, a child of
disbelief and doubt up until now and will be even (I know this) to

the grave. What horrible torment this thirst to believe has cost me and continues to cost me, a thirst that is all the stronger in my soul the more negative arguments there are in me" (end of January-third week of February, 1854; *Complete Letters* 1: 194). Yet in the same letter the writer concludes that he has found in himself a "symbol of faith" in which all is clear, and that symbol is "to believe that there is nothing more beautiful, more profound, more attractive, more wise, more courageous and more perfect than Christ [...] Moreover, if someone proved to me that Christ were outside the truth, and it *really* were that the truth lay outside Christ, I would prefer to remain with Christ rather than with the truth" (*Complete Letters* 1: 195).

The conflict between Dostoevsky's belief in the beauty of Christ and his understanding of the power of his contemporaries' attacks on religion and the idea of God forms a powerful undercurrent in the great novels he wrote in the 1860s and 1870s, and his major works often center upon a man who is torn between intellectual skepticism about the existence of God and a haunting desire to know the truth and perhaps even to believe. But this conflict is not waged simply on a philosophical plane. Often in Dostoevsky's work, it exhibits a profound connection to issues of social justice and human happiness. From his first years in the Engineering Academy Dostoevsky had been captivated by the social humanitarianism that was sweeping into Russia from the West (through the writings of Victor Hugo, among others). Not long thereafter, Dostoevsky fell under the influence of the prominent critic Vissarion Belinsky, who evolved, in the words of the Dostoevsky scholar Joseph Frank, from championing a form of utopian socialism "informed by Christian moral-religious values" to a position that was more "militantly antireligious" (*Dostoevsky: A Writer in His Time*, 120, 121). How far Dostoevsky actually went in following Belinsky is not entirely clear. Dostoevsky was surely moved to indignation by the evidence of social injustice he observed in contemporary Russia, but it is less certain that he ever truly embraced the atheism that was now being advanced by some of his more radical acquaintances. When he stood on the scaffold awaiting what he believed would be his execution, he turned to a fellow prisoner, Nikolay Speshnev, and declared: "*Nous serons avec le Christ*" ["We shall be with Christ"], to which the atheist Speshnev responded: "*Un peu de poussière*" ["A bit of dust"].[2]

According to Dostoevsky, his experience in prison camp allowed him to appreciate in a new way a profound reservoir of spirituality in the Russian people.[3] As the years went on, he became ever more convinced that a significant factor in Russia's rising social and political unrest was the estrangement of the educated population from the great masses of the Russian peasantry.

After returning to St. Petersburg in 1859, Dostoevsky became aware of how dramatically the ideological arena of the leading intellectuals and writers had changed over the last decade. An enthusiasm for science and scientific discovery had captured the imagination of the progressive intelligentsia. Materialism, positivism, utilitarianism were the watchwords of the day. One of the more influential texts circulating among the intellectuals was an essay by Nikolay Chernyshevsky entitled "The Anthropological Principle in Philosophy" (1860). Greatly impressed with the discoveries being made in the natural sciences, Chernyshevsky asserted that equivalent "facts and laws" would be discovered in "the moral sciences" as well (*Selected Philosophical Essays*, 92–3). All human conduct can be explained by discoverable natural causes. Therefore, the concept of individual free will is an illusion, and humans are bound to act out of pure self-interest, which, they will ultimately discover, must be aligned with the interests of the whole society.

Having become intensely familiar with acts of irrationality and "free will" in prison camp, Dostoevsky took issue with Chernyshevsky's reductionist theories, and in his *Notes from the Underground* he chose as his narrator-protagonist a man who has absorbed these theories but who, paradoxically, refuses to accept their apparent implications. The underground man declares that people may sometime act in ways that are injurious to themselves, simply to show that they remain individuals with a will of their own. As he puts it: "all of man's purpose, it seems to me, really consists of nothing but proving to himself every moment that he is a man and not an organ stop! Proving it even at the cost of his own skin; even at the cost of turning into a troglodyte" (*Notes*, 35). This underground man himself, however, is deeply unhappy. Paralyzed by self-consciousness, he is unable to act or to reach out to another person. Dostoevsky had originally intend to suggest that Christianity might offer a way out of the underground man's dilemma, but the censors made him remove that element of the text. He never restored it. However, in his next novel, *Crime and Punishment*, in which Dostoevsky again sought to rebut the influence of Chernyshevsky's ideas on self-interest and rational egoism (displayed also in Chernyshevsky's novel *What Is To Be Done?* [1863]), he was allowed to introduce the Christian ideals of forgiveness and redemption to counter Raskolnikov's bitterness and despair, and from this point on the battle between these ideals and the tenets of radical atheism would be waged in earnest on the pages of his work.

Although Dostoevsky believed that the self-sacrificing conduct of Christ could serve as a model for human behavior, he also perceived the difficulty humans face in adopting this model. In an extraordinary set of notes he made after the death of his first wife, he wrote: "To love a person *as oneself*, according to Christ's commandment, is impossible [...] The *I* is an obstacle. Only Christ was able to do it, but Christ was an eternal ideal toward which man strives." Nonetheless, after Christ's appearance on earth, the ultimate goal of the individual must be "to annihilate this *I*, to give it over completely to each and to all, undividedly and selflessly [...] This is Christ's heaven."[4] Many of Dostoevsky's fictional characters in the 1860s and 1870s strive mightily to overcome the demands of their egos and to serve others, yet one can find in almost every one of his novels a clear example of selflessness and self-sacrifice.

During the 1870s Dostoevsky became steadily more concerned about Russia's future and the role of Russia's youth in shaping that future. Keenly aware of their idealism (seen, for example, in the movement of "going to the people" in the mid-1870s), he worried that they might fail to embrace the spirituality that he saw as an integral attribute of the Russian people. His entries in *A Writer's Diary* argue repeatedly about the need to overcome the estrangement between the values of the urban intelligentsia and the common people. His writing was becoming increasingly messianic (and xenophobic) about Russia's mission in the world. The events surrounding the Russo-Turkish War of 1877–78 were treated by Dostoevsky in apocalyptic terms. Never was he more convinced that Russia and the Russian idea were destined to play a unique role in world affairs.

Dostoevsky was bolstered in these reflections by his acquaintance with the brilliant young philosopher and poet Vladimir Solovyov (1853–1900). They had become acquainted in the early 1870s, and after the death of Dostoevsky's son Alexey in May 1878, Solovyov accompanied Dostoevsky on a pilgrimage to the Optyna Pustyn' monastery in June 1878. Dostoevsky later incorporated impressions from this trip into his description of the monastery and its inhabitants in *The Brothers Karamazov*. Dostoevsky found in Solovyov a thinker whose ideas on religion and on Russia harmonized with his own. In the January 1877 issue of *A Writer's Diary*, Dostoevsky disparaged both Catholicism and Protestantism, and declared that "meanwhile, in the East, the third world idea—the Slavic idea, a new idea that is coming into being—has truly caught ablaze and has begun to cast a light that has never before been seen; it is, perhaps, the third future possibility for settling the destinies of Europe and of humanity." This "Russian idea," as he calls it, is the idea of "the unity of all humanity" (*Writer's Diary* 2: 815, 830). To realize this idea, each Russian "must become Russian above all," and must stop despising the Russian people (*Writer's Diary* 2: 833). Just a few months later, Solovyov was articulating similar views in a speech entitled "Three Forces." Proclaiming that the "great historical calling of Russia [...] is a religious calling in the highest sense of this word," Solovyov argues that the Russian nation can serve as an intermediary between humanity and the divine world, and that to make this possible, there must be "the awakening of a *positive consciousness* of the Russian nation." To achieve that end, the Russian intelligentsia must restore in themselves "the Russian national character" (*Enemies from the East?*, 33).

Although Solovyov did not share Dostoevsky's theories on Russian nationalism in all its particulars,[5] one concept held a central place in both men's view of human potential: the concept of Godmanhood. Solovyov gave a series of lectures on the subject of Godmanhood in St. Petersburg early in 1878, and Dostoevsky attended these lectures faithfully. Solovyov perceived a split between traditional faith (faith in God) and modern secular faith (faith in man), and he argued that these two faiths could be reconciled through the "unique, complete, and integral truth of Godmanhood" (*Lectures on Godmanhood*, 85). Dostoevsky's works are full of characters who have rejected the notion of God (but who sometimes remain tormented about the question of God's existence), and have sought to put themselves in the place formerly occupied by God. They strive to become the Man-god, and they value their intellectual power and their will above all else. Yet these characters inevitably end up destroying themselves or others. In place of freedom, they find only a void, and they are crushed by anger or despair. The solution, for Dostoevsky as for Solovyov, lay in the figure of Jesus Christ. In Christ are united both God and man, and the model of loving self-sacrifice displayed in Christ's life shone as a bright beacon for Dostoevsky, whose own "hosanna," he asserted while writing *The Brothers Karamazov*, had "passed through a great crucible of doubts" (*PSS* 27: 86).

In fact, Dostoevsky instills into *The Brothers Karamazov* both his greatest affirmation of faith and his greatest challenge to that faith. The conflict between doubt and faith is nowhere more evident than in the conflict between the ideas put forth by the intellectual skeptic Ivan Karamazov and those offered by the spiritually devout Father Zosima. About Book Five, in which Ivan torments Alyosha with his stories of child abuse and questions the justice of God's universe, Dostoevsky wrote to his editor, N. A. Lyubimov: "this Book 5 is, in my view, the culminating point of the novel and it has to be finished up with special care. Its idea, as you will see from the text I've sent, is the portrayal of extreme blasphemy and the seed of the idea of destruction of our time in Russia among young people divorced from reality." Dostoevsky goes further: "My hero takes up a theme that I *think* irrefutable—the senselessness of the suffering of children—and he derives from it the absurdity of all historical reality" (10 May 1879; *Complete Letters* 5: 83).

Although Dostoevsky declared that Ivan's argument is "irrefutable," he strove mightily to counter its force and validity both in the following book, Book Six, and in the novel as a whole. Of his task he wrote: "My protagonist's blasphemy [...] will be solemnly refuted in the following (June) issue, for which I am now working with fear, trepidation, and reverence, since I consider my task (the rout of anarchism) a civic feat." (*Complete Letters* 5: 83). A month later he wrote to Lyubimov again, and this time he addresses his work on the portrait of Father Zosima more directly: "If I manage it, I'll do a good thing: *I'll force people to recognize* that a pure, ideal Christian is not an abstract matter, but one graphically real, possible, standing right before our eyes, and that Christianity is the Russian Land's only refuge from all its evils. I pray God that I manage it" (11 June 1879; *Complete Letters* 5: 89). Yet once he had written Book Six, he was still not sure whether he had succeeded in his goal. As he wrote to K. P. Pobedonostsev: "I tremble for it in the sense of whether it will be a *sufficient* reply." Part of his concern, as he expressed it to Pobedonostsev, was that the "reply" he provides "is not a direct one, not [...] point by point, but only an indirect one. Here something directly opposed to the above-stated worldview is offered, but again, it is offered not point by point, but so to speak, in an artistic picture" (24 August 1879; *Complete Letters* 5: 154–5). Ultimately, as Dostoevsky himself understood, he would not be refuting Ivan with a simple set of polemical responses. Rather, as he wrote in his journal, "*the whole novel* serves as an answer" to Ivan's denial of God (*PSS* 27: 48). Of course, the question of whether Dostoevsky *did* succeed in his quest is one the readers of the novel have been debating with passion from the moment it first saw the light of day.

The Brothers Karamazov and Russian literature

The Brothers Karamazov represents the culmination of Dostoevsky's career as a writer. As such, it displays an intricate synthesis of themes, images, and motifs from Russian and world literature and from Dostoevsky's own personal storehouse of concerns and techniques. Dostoevsky read voraciously and widely throughout his life. From his youth onwards, he would be inspired by writers such as Schiller, Hugo, the English Gothic novelists, Sir Walter Scott, Shakespeare, Poe, Goethe, Hoffmann, George Sand, and many, many others. In his fiction, he sometimes emulated the plot structures or character types found in world literature, and he often invoked prior models in order to overturn or rebut their apparent messages. *The Brothers Karamazov* contains numerous quotations from or allusions to works of world literature, often with an ironic or parodic twist. Dostoevsky would use such quotations as a means of characterizing the main figures in the book: a quotation from Schiller, for example, might demonstrate a character's Romantic leanings, while an association with Voltaire might suggest a character's naïveté or skepticism. Quotations from the Bible play a special role in the text. When a figure such as Father Zosima quotes a Biblical text, the utterance carries the weight of absolute authority. When the corrupt Fyodor Karamazov quotes from the Bible, however, he often distorts the quotation, and this shows the reader something meaningful about Fyodor's own twisted personality.

As important as references to world literature are in *The Brothers Karamazov*, Dostoevsky was above all a Russian writer, and his novel reflects his intense awareness of developments in Russian literature, culture, and society. Perhaps the most important Russian writer for Dostoevsky was Alexander Pushkin. In fact, the critic Nina Perlina has argued that after the Bible, Pushkin's "poetic word" is the second most authoritative source of literary quotation in *The Brothers Karamazov* (*Varieties of Poetic Utterance*, 25). In the speech he delivered at the celebration of the unveiling of the Pushkin monument in Moscow in 1880 (when he was still in the final stages of writing *The Brothers Karamazov*), Dostoevsky called Pushkin "a prophecy and a revelation," and he provided striking interpretations of Pushkin's narrative poem *The Gypsies* and his novel in verse *Eugene Onegin*: for Dostoevsky, Pushkin's depiction of the protagonist revealed important truths about the Russian national character. While the male heroes reflect the fundamental alienation of the educated Russian gentry from their native land (an alienation that Dostoevsky feared was continuing to plague contemporary Russia), the figure of Tatiana in *Eugene Onegin* represents a shining model of strength, beauty, and the willingness to sacrifice one's own happiness for the happiness of others.

Yet it is not just the symbolic significance of Pushkin's characters that Dostoevsky wished to bring to the attention of his audience. In his view, Pushkin had the unique quality of "embodying himself fully within another nationality" (*Writer's Diary* 2: 1292). This very universalism, Dostoevsky argues, is a quintessential characteristic of the Russian national spirit itself. As he put it: "Indeed, the mission of the Russian is unquestionably pan-European and universal. To become a real Russian, to become completely Russian, perhaps means just [...] to become brother to all people, *a panhuman*, if you like" (*Writer's Diary* 2: 1294). In the concluding portion of his speech, Dostoevsky moves on from Pushkin to speak of the mission of Russia herself: future Russians, he asserts, "will realize [...] that to become a genuine Russian will mean specifically: to strive to bring an ultimate reconciliation to Europe's contradictions, to indicate that the solution to Europe's anguish is to be found in the panhuman and all-unifying Russian soul [...] and at last, perhaps, to utter the ultimate word of great, general harmony, ultimate brotherly accord of all tribes through the law of Christ's Gospel!" (*Writer's Diary* 2: 1294). Dostoevsky's speech met with tremendous success, and he incorporated several of its central themes as well as the very act of oratory into the text of *The Brothers Karamazov*.

Dostoevsky also reacted strongly to the literary creations of other writers of his day. His response to the writings of Nikolay Chernyshevsky has been discussed in the previous section. Other Russian writers whose work interested Dostoevsky were the poet Nikolay Nekrasov (1821–78) and the prose writers Ivan Turgenev (1818–83) and Leo Tolstoy (1828–1910). Dostoevsky contrasted the difficult conditions he worked under with that of his more affluent contemporaries: "I'm convinced that not one of our writers, past or living, wrote under the conditions in which I *constantly* write. Turgenev would die from the very thought" (17 June 1866; *Complete Letters* 2: 200). More important, however, was his response to the major themes of their work. One topic of central significance to Dostoevsky as he worked on *The Brothers Karamazov* was the state of the Russian family as depicted in the literature of the day. Dostoevsky perceived the representation of the family in Turgenev and Tolstoy to be a rarified phenomenon reflective of an affluent gentry lifestyle and threatened by the forces of change that were sweeping across Russian society. As he saw it, the Russian family was in danger of fragmentation and dissolution in the second half of the nineteenth century. Reacting to the suicide of a twelve-year-old boy, Dostoevsky wrote in his *Writer's Diary* in January 1877 that this event exhibited "features of a new sort of reality quite different from that of the placid, middle-stratum Moscow landowning family [...] whose *historian* is our Count Leo Tolstoy [...] One cannot deny that a way of life in Russia is disintegrating; consequently, family life disintegrates as well" (*Writer's Diary* 2: 847). He wonders who the new "historian" will be who can illuminate this chaos.

In his late fiction, Dostoevsky contemplated being just such a historian. His novel *The Adolescent* depicts a profound estrangement between fathers and sons, and he includes at the end of the text a commentary provided by someone to whom the narrator had shown the work. This commentary expresses concisely Dostoevsky's own views of the changes occurring in the Russian family. Speaking of the family depicted in the novel, the commentator writes: "if you could convince me, Arkady, that this family is an exception, an accident, I would be very relieved. But wouldn't it be much more accurate to conclude that many such legitimate Russian families are broken up and become *accidental* groupings, all merging into the general disorder and chaos. In your manuscript there emerges a type of such an *accidental family*" (*Adolescent*, 565).

Trying to get at the underlying source for the "accidental" quality of the modern family, Dostoevsky looked first and foremost to the role of the father in the family. In the July–August 1871 issue of his *Writer's Diary*, Dostoevsky repeated the assertion that the "contemporary Russian family is becoming more and more an *accidental* family" and he went on to explain his usage of this term: "People will ask what this *accidental nature* is and what I mean by these words. I reply that in my opinion the accidental nature of today's Russian family consists in the loss among contemporary fathers of any common idea about their families—an idea common to all fathers that binds them together, an idea in which they could believe and could teach their children to believe" (*Writer's Diary* 2: 1034, 1041).

In drawing attention to the father–child relationship, and the importance of fathers passing binding values on to their children, Dostoevsky touches upon a significant theme in nineteenth-century Russian literature: the so-called "Fathers and Sons" theme. The theme takes its name from Ivan Turgenev's most famous novel, *Fathers and Sons* (1862). Turgenev centered his novel on two young men who seem to have rejected the values of their parents' generation. Yet while one of the young men, the nihilist Evgeny Bazarov, dies at the end of the novel, the other, Arkady Kirsanov, gets married and settles down in a lifestyle that is very much like that of the older generation.

The fathers-and-children theme played a major role in Dostoevsky's work as well. In his novel *The Devils* he depicts the pernicious consequences of parents' defective upbringing of their children. Stepan Verkhovensky, an idle liberal representing the generation of the 1840s in Russia, has had a doubly negative impact on the younger generation. He sent his own son, Pyotr, away to be raised by relatives in a distant province, and in his capacity as tutor to Nikolay Stavrogin, he seemed to have over-stimulated the child's imagination with inappropriate confessions and intimacies. His liberal teachings left the representatives of the younger generation without a stable foundation to sustain them during periods of personal difficulty or doubt.

In March 1876 Dostoevsky jotted down a few notes for a novel with the working title of *Fathers and Sons* (*Ottsy i deti*, which literally translates as *Fathers and Children*), but he never fulfilled his plans (*PSS* 17: 6–8).[6] Instead, he put his energies into *The Brothers Karamazov*, setting at the center of the novel a family in full-blown crisis. Fyodor, the patriarch of the Karamazov clan, is a selfish, avaricious, and cynical man who literally "forgot" his children when they were little, so that they had to be taken care of by others, initially by Fyodor's servant and later by the boys' relatives. The boys' mothers were absent too: one ran away from Fyodor and later died; the second wife died after only a few years of marriage. Dostoevsky had the utmost sympathy for the wellbeing of children, and the neglect or abuse of a child was, in his eyes, the greatest sin. It has often been noted that each of the three sons seems to display one prominent aspect of the human personality: Dmitry represents the body or senses, Ivan the intellect, and Alyosha the spirit. Through this structure one can detect something like the fragmentation of the integral personality, a fragmentation that reflects the lack of wholeness or unity afflicting the Karamazov family itself. What is more, rumor has it that one of the Karamazov's servants, Pavel Smerdyakov, is actually a *fourth* son, the illegitimate offspring of Fyodor and a mentally deficient homeless woman; this illegitimacy strikingly highlights the aura of dissolution and degeneration that permeates the Karamazov household. Smerdyakov simmers with a brooding rancor about the way he is viewed in the Karamazov family, and this rancor, together with anger and resentment felt by some of the other brothers toward their father, ultimately culminates in the brutal murder of the father, a murder for which all the sons can be said to bear at least some responsibility.

Faced with the growing crisis in family relationships in Russia, Dostoevsky was of course interested in the question of how the family could be mended, or how new families could be formed on stronger, more enduring bases. One thinker whose writing on this issue intrigued Dostoevsky was Nikolay Fyodorov (1828–1903). Dostoevsky was sent a summary of Fyodorov's teachings by one of the philosopher's followers, and Dostoevsky read it with great interest and sympathy. Fyodorov perceived the contemporary world to be striven with conflict and division. He argued that the world must overcome this divisiveness by coming together in a spirit of kinship, with the primary task of the sons being the resurrection of their dead fathers. Once the forefathers have been resurrected, humanity can form a broad, universal family on the model of the Holy Trinity that unites God the Father, the Son, and the Holy Spirit. Although Fyodorov's program was highly speculative and utopian, Dostoevsky was drawn to his emphasis on overcoming family divisions and establishing a new relationship between sons and their fathers. In one of his notebook entries for *The Brothers Karamazov* Dostoevsky wrote: "*The resurrection of our ancestors* depends on us" (*Notebooks*, 32). Depicting in *The Brothers Karamazov* a set of sons who feel murderous rage toward their father, the writer sought an antidote to this rage in a spirit of forgiveness and love, with brotherly love replacing inadequate or damaged paternal and filial love.[7] Over the course of the novel one finds a range of responses to the problem of inadequate or absent fathers, from violent rebellion against fathers perceived to be unjust or abusive to a search for a surrogate father who can provide love and support. Ultimately in Dostoevsky's novel, behind the search for an adequate father on earth looms a deeper yearning—for God, the Father in heaven. Dostoevsky's entire novel provides an illuminating exploration of this central quest.

Notes

1 See Andrei Dostoevskii, *Vospominaniia Andreia Mikhailovicha Dostoevskogo*, 63.

2 F. N. L'vov, "Zapiska o dele petrashevtsev," 188.

3 See Dostoevsky's story "The Peasant Marei" ("Muzhik Marei") for his account of what one might call a conversion experience, although the work was written much later than the events described and therefore may reflect subsequent developments within Dostoevsky himself. On this, see R. L. Jackson, "The Triple Vision: 'The Peasant Marei,'" in *The Art of Dostoevsky: Deliriums and Nocturnes*, 20–32.

4 Quoted in Steven Cassedy, *Dostoevsky's Religion*, 116.

5 For a discussion of this topic, see Marina Kostalevsky, *Dostoevsky and Soloviev: The Art of Integral Vision*, 134–44.

6 For a discussion of Dostoevsky's depiction of troubled families in his late work, see Susanne Fusso, *Discovering Sexuality in Dostoevsky*, 101–18; and W. J. Leatherbarrow, *Fyodor Dostoyevsky: The Brothers Karamazov*, 21–30.

7 Anna A. Berman writes persuasively about the importance of brotherly (or lateral) love as opposed to paternal (or hierarchical) love in the novel ("Siblings in *The Brothers Karamazov*").

CHAPTER TWO

Language, form, and style

Voices in dialogue

Leo Tolstoy was famous for the declarative pronouncements he made in his fiction. *Anna Karenina* begins with the memorable line: "All happy families resemble one another, but each unhappy family is unhappy in its own way" (*Anna Karenina*, 1). In Tolstoy's work, the author is the true sovereign of the world he has created; characters and events are clearly subordinated to his perspective on events. With Dostoevsky, however, the situation is often more complex. Studying Dostoevsky's narrative technique, the Russian literary critic Mikhail Bakhtin declared Dostoevsky to be a "polyphonic" author. That is, Dostoevsky seemed to endow many of his central characters with distinct voices of their own and allowed them to make the case for their worldviews on an equal footing with each other. As Bakhtin put it: "*A plurality of independent and unmerged voices and consciousnesses, a genuine polyphony of full valid voices is in fact the chief characteristic of Dostoevsky's novels*" (*Problems of Dostoevsky's Poetics*, 6).

Bakhtin perceived that Dostoevsky's authorial position is only one of several that are engaged in a dialogic relationship with each other. Although one can usually make out what Dostoevsky's own position on an issue might be (and he sometimes has a fictional character articulate his ideas for him), each character is allowed to express his individual perspective with passion, determination, and significant autonomy. What is more, as Robin Feuer Miller has pointed out, "[t]he primary unit of interest for Dosteovsky always involves characters in relationship to others—victim and victimizer, confesser and confessor—or in dialogue with themselves" (The Brothers Karamazov: *Worlds of the Novel*, 61). The reader too may become drawn into this dialogue and must wrestle with the clash of ideas and worldviews that the text presents.

In *The Brothers Karamazov* this polyphonic principle is on full display. Each of the three Karamazov brothers has a specific orientation on life that gives him a unique place within the family structure and makes him indelibly memorable to the reader of the novel. Dmitry, the eldest, embodies the emotional and sensual side of human nature: he is drawn to beauty, especially female beauty, and he is willing to degrade himself if necessary to fulfill his desires. Ivan, the second son, is the intellectual of the family. He uses his reasoning faculties to probe the mysteries of life and to question the justice of God's universe. Alyosha, the youngest son, is oriented toward the spiritual world. He entered the monastery seeking an escape from the darkness of everyday life into the light of the spiritual life. This is not to say that each of the brothers is devoid of the traits that predominate in his siblings. Ivan and Alyosha both have their sensual sides, and a concern with the existence and agency of God burns within all of them.[1] Combined together, the three seem to make up what Konstantin Mochulsky calls an "organically collective personality" (*Dostoevsky*, 598), but the very fact that these basic human elements—emotions, intellect, spirituality—are divided up in this way points to a state of fragmentation or dissolution within the family that is one of the major concerns of the novel itself. Then too, rumor has it that the young servant in the Karamazov household, Pavel Smerdyakov, is the illegitimate son of the family patriarch Fyodor, and indeed, this fourth brother, tainted as he his by association with the demonic, represents what might be called the "shadow" part of the collective self, that part of the personality representing everything that one feels uncomfortable about and would wish push away from oneself.[2]

Dostoevsky provides each of these characters with the opportunity to express his attitude toward the world around him in clear and compelling terms. Indeed, in a Dostoevsky novel, characters seem only truly alive when they are involved in a vital relationship with another and able to remain open to the other's voice. Many scenes in *The Brothers Karamazov* feature characters in urgent conversation with one another, revealing their cherished thoughts and anxiously awaiting their interlocutor's reaction. As the novel unfolds, the reader has the opportunity to evaluate the merit of these positions not only in terms of the ideas they contain, but also in terms of the consequences that arise when they are carried out. Moreover, each character's voice has its own unique intonations, accents, and even favored vocabulary. The speeches of the monk Zosima, for example, often display traces of his ecclesiastic orientation, with numerous archaisms and Church Slavonicisms.[3] Dostoevsky was highly conscious of what he was doing, and he explained as much to his editor, Nikolay Lyubimov. Writing of Zosima, he declared: "Although I quite share the ideas that he expresses, if I personally were expressing them, *on my own behalf*, I would express them in a different form and a different language. He, however, *could not* have expressed himself in either a language or a *spirit* other than the one I gave him. Otherwise an artistic personage wouldn't be created" (7 August 1879; *Complete Letters* 5: 130–1). The same holds true for other characters, such as the German-born doctor who speaks with a prominent German accent, or the peasant driver whose speech is riddled with colloquialisms. Even silences can be pregnant with meaning in the novel. Some of the most important moments in the work occur when characters refrain from words (which may be overly laden with multiple meanings) and resort simply to gestures.[4] All of these linguistic and stylistic effects add to the vibrancy and vitality of Dostoevsky's text.

The role of quotation

A significant role in the novel is given to quotation. Very often, one character will articulate an idea or phrase, and a second or third character will repeat that idea or phrase, now giving it his or her own twist, so that key words, images, and concepts pick up a complex set of overtones that increase the richness and depth of the overall text. An interesting example of this occurs in the second chapter of Book Five, when Alyosha is looking for his brother Dmitry and he asks Smerdyakov: "Will brother Dmitry soon be back?" To which Smerdyakov replies: "How am I to know about Dmitry Fyodorovich? It's not as if I were his keeper"

(196). The reader will recognize in Smerdyakov's response an echo of the famous answer Cain delivered to God after Cain had killed his brother Abel and God asked him where his brother Abel was. Cain responded: "I do not know. Am I my brother's keeper?" (Gen. 4.9). Smerdyakov's response not only associates him with Cain, the first murderer of the human race, but it also reminds the reader of Smerdyakov's potential sensitivity to the issue of his place in the Karamazov family. He undoubtedly assumes that he is Fyodor's illegitimate son, and therefore he is Dmitry's half-brother, yet he has always been treated only as a servant, and this status surely rankles him.

Nevertheless, Smerdyakov does tell Alyosha that Ivan Fyodorovich was hoping to dine with Dmitry in a tavern in the marketplace, and when Alyosha arrives at the tavern, he asks Ivan what he thinks will result from the enmity between Dmitry and their father Fyodor. Ivan replies: "What have I to do with it? Am I my brother Dmitry's keeper?" (200). Ivan immediately catches himself, and acknowledges that he is echoing Cain's response about Abel. But he then continues to reject any responsibility for either Dmitry or his father, and declares that he is leaving town. In this scene, the reader recognizes that not only is Ivan plagiarizing from the murderous Cain, but he unknowingly echoes the sinister Smerdyakov as well, and he accentuates this aura of malevolence by invoking the devil twice during his utterance ("chert voz'mi" ["the devil take it"] and "chert" [literally, "devil," but perhaps more readily translated as "damn"]).

The concept of "plagiarism" carries important weight in *The Brothers Karamazov*, because *whom* one quotes may be as important as the quotation itself. When Alyosha repeats the words of Father Zosima, it is an indication of acceptance of beneficent wisdom. But when he repeats one of Ivan's expressions, as in a scene in a cemetery when he is plunged into despair over the fact that Zosima's death triggers a scandal rather than the wonders that Alyosha thinks are only fitting for such a magnificent being (Book Seven, Chapter Two), the reader realizes how strongly Ivan's pernicious influence has affected the impressionable youth.

Quotations from the Bible and from literary sources also play an important role in *The Brothers Karamazov*. The critic Nina Perlina has argued that there is a hierarchical system of quotations in the novel. At the top of the hierarchy stands the Bible: "It is a legacy of absolute, incontestable authority" (*Varieties of Poetic Utterance*, 24). When used by figures such as Father Zosima, Biblical quotation can have significant instructional value for those to whom it is delivered. We see this in Zosima's interactions with the peasant women who seek him out in Book Two, Chapter Three, and we see it again when Zosima helps a murderer troubled by his conscience to arrive at the decision to confess and take responsibility for his crime (Book Six, Chapter Two). Significantly, one of the Biblical quotations that Zosima shows to his visitor is the passage from the Gospel of St. John that reads: "Verily, verily, I say unto you, except a corn of wheat fall into the ground and die, it abideth alone: but if it die, it bringeth forth much fruit" (12.24). This passage, with its agricultural metaphor and its message of death and resurrection, resonates powerfully throughout the novel, and this will be explored further below.

In Dostoevsky's works, however, few things are one-dimensional. And just as Biblical quotation can be used for positive, edifying purposes, so too can it be used for pernicious, even blasphemous purposes. Indeed, how a character uses Biblical quotation can tell the reader quite a bit about that character's personality and intentions. A good example of this occurs in Book Two, Chapter Six, when the Karamazov family gathers in Father Zosima's monastery cell to discuss the conflict between Dmitry and Fyodor. Fyodor, ever eager to stir up a scandal, says in reference to Grushenka's youthful affair with an older man: "She fell perhaps in her youth, ruined by her environment, but she loved much, and Christ forgave the woman 'who loved much'" (69). One of the monks objects that it was not for such a love that Christ gave forgiveness, but Fyodor sticks to his position, and abuses the monks further. Of course, Fyodor has misappropriated the Biblical quotation. In its original usage (Luke 7.47), Jesus speaks about a woman who showed her love for him by washing his feet with her tears, drying them with her hair, and anointing him with oil. Grushenka's affair with an older man is of an entirely different character.

A similar distortion of a Gospel text occurs in Ivan's story of the Grand Inquisitor's encounter with Christ in sixteenth-century Spain. Ivan's Grand Inquisitor reproaches Jesus for not succumbing to the temptations of the devil during his forty-day trial in the wilderness, and he refers to the way Jesus rebuffed the devil's suggestion that Jesus turn bread into stones: "Thou didst reply that man lives not by bread alone" (219), but although he conveys the first part of Jesus's response correctly, the Inquisitor omits the second part. In the original Biblical passage, Jesus asserts: "It is written, that man shall not live by bread alone, but by every word that proceeds from the mouth of God" (Mt. 4.4). Ivan, through the Grand Inquisitor, omits the important message of Jesus's retort: that the word of God provides the true sustenance that men and women need. The Grand Inquisitor's (and Ivan's) consistent elision of God and his word signals a desire to downplay the influence and significance of God in human affairs.

Quotations from the Bible are not the only form of quotation that appears prominently in *The Brothers Karamazov*. One can find direct quotations from and allusions to many secular writers as well, from the German poet Friedrich Schiller to Russian writers such as Nikolay Nekrasov or Alexander Herzen. Again, Nina Perlina has asserted that the poetic word of Alexander Pushkin is the second most important element in the hierarchy established by Dostoevsky in his novel (*Varieties of Poetic Utterance*, 25). As with Biblical citations, the way a character quotes (or misquotes) a passage from Pushkin's work can impart important information about that character's background or intentions. Examples range from the schoolboy Kolya Krasotkin's uninformed reference to the Russian critic Vissarion Belinsky's criticism of Pushkin's treatment of the character of Tatiana in *Eugene Onegin* (which Kolya himself has not even read in the original) to a complex allusion to a late Pushkin poem, "Desert fathers and pure women...," that crops up in Ivan's encounter with his devil in Book Eleven. The devil claims that he wishes to sow a seed of faith in Ivan, a seed that will grow into an oak tree so strong that Ivan, sitting on it, will long to join the "desert fathers and chaste women" (543). The devil's words seem highly parodic, for the poem from which he draws offers a serenely beautiful paraphrase of a prayer of St. Ephraim the Syrian, and its calm supplication for humility, patience, and love seem far removed both from the devil's frivolous chatter and Ivan's rebellious soul. Yet the underlying spirit of the poem may in fact resonate with Ivan's own tortured longing for faith and reconciliation, and thus the impression of parody it evokes upon first reading masks a deeper seriousness dwelling beneath the surface.

In some cases, even a single word can accumulate substantial meaning as it is repeated from speaker to speaker. The word *umnyi* ("intelligent," "clever," "wise") offers an apt example. While the word is occasionally in a neutral way at the outset of the novel, it takes on a distinctive charge when it first appears in Ivan's story about the Grand Inquisitor (Book Five, Chapter Five). Introducing the topic of the devil's three temptations of Jesus in the wilderness, the Grand Inquisitor refers to the devil as the "dread and intelligent spirit" (219), and he uses that epithet later in his speech as well. The Grand Inquisitor deems the devil to be "intelligent," because, as the Grand Inquisitor sees it, the devil understood humanity's essential weakness and indicated to Jesus that one could secure people's loyalty through the formula of *"miracle, mystery, and authority"* (223). The Grand Inquisitor himself, Ivan declares, perceived that Jesus's expectations that humanity would follow him freely were too lofty for humanity, so the Grand Inquisitor "turned back and joined—the intelligent people" (227). Listening to this, Alyosha objects that these so-called "intelligent" people offer nothing but atheism, and Ivan acknowledges that this might be so. Yet Ivan finds great tragedy in the Grand Inquisitor's scheme of deception.

Through this passage, Dostoevsky has established a link between the word "intelligent" and atheism, allegiance to the devil, and so on. Significantly, these associations are carried over to Ivan's very next conversation, which he conducts with Smerdyakov. Ivan sees Smerdyakov standing outside his father's house, and he realizes that Smerdyakov wishes to speak with him. As he looks at Smerdyakov, he notices that Smerdyakov's left eye seems to wink and grin as if saying: "Where are you going? You won't pass by; you see that we two intelligent people have something to say to each other" (232). A moment later, when Smerdyakov smiles, Ivan again thinks he detects in Smerdyakov's left eye a hint that Ivan should understand what Smerdyakov is talking about if he is "an intelligent man" (232). Ivan might be projecting this unspoken message onto Smerdyakov, but the use of the epithet "intelligent" (*umnyi*) recalls for the reader the demonic associations established for the word in the story Ivan has just narrated about the Grand Inquisitor. The gist of the conversation is that if Ivan were to depart for the nearby town of Chermashnya, his father Fyodor would be unprotected and could be murdered by Dmitry. On the next day, Ivan tells Smerdyakov that he will go to Chermashnya on an errand for his father, and Smerdyakov makes a surprising declaration: "It's a true saying then, that 'it's always interesting speaking with an intelligent man'" (241). Smerdyakov's use of the word "intelligent" here is curious, for it seems that he has somehow picked up on Ivan's internal speculations about what Smerdyakov's left eye was saying, or that Ivan's perceptions were precisely accurate in some mysterious way. Most importantly of all, it connects Smerdyakov with the associations developed around the "intelligent spirit" of the wilderness and the "intelligent people" the Grand Inquisitor has joined after abandoning Jesus. Smerdyakov's utterance is so remarkable that Ivan ponders it as he drives away: "Why is it interesting speaking with an intelligent man? What did he mean by that?" (241–2). Ivan is troubled by his feeling that he may have entered into some unspoken contract with Smerdyakov, and he ends up by calling himself a scoundrel.

After Fyodor has been murdered and Dmitry has been charged with the crime, Ivan is plagued with doubt about his potential role in the murder—did he allow it to happen? did he encourage it?—and so he seeks Smerdyakov out to try to settle the issue. In their first two encounters, the phrase "it's always interesting speaking with an intelligent man" comes up several times (510, 512, 519), and it becomes clear that the phrase encapsulates the entire concept of Fyodor's murder and Ivan's implicit involvement. Yet the word "intelligent" and the sinister associations that have been developed around the word are not confined simply to the Ivan–Smerdyakov relationship. It turns out that these sinister associations have spread outward, and now affect other characters in the novel, most notably the shifty figure named Rakitin, who has been assaulting Dmitry in jail with all kinds of theories laced with socialism and atheism. Dmitry tells Alyosha that Rakitin is "an intelligent man," and he repeats the word "intelligent" (495). Dmitry goes on to tell Alyosha that when he tried to counter Rakitin's atheism with a question about how people can have morality without God, Rakitin cynically responded: "an intelligent man can do what he likes" (497). By this point in the novel, the word "intelligent" carries clear connotations of sinister godlessness, and Rakitin's endorsement of the formula that for an intelligent man, everything is permitted, indicates that he belongs squarely in the camp of Smerdyakov and the Grand Inquisitor. One can find numerous other examples of key words and images that carry such significant associations.

Narrators and narratives

The main narrator of *The Brothers Karamazov* is an indistinct figure. He seems to be an inhabitant of the town in which the central events take place (he makes reference to "our district" [11]) and he himself attends the trial of Dmitry Karamazov which caps the main part of the novel. Yet although he can be quite chatty, and does not hesitate to repeat the gossip and rumors that swirl around his town, he appears to be curiously inconsistent in his knowledge and presentation of many of those events. At times, he provides the reader with intimate details about a character's feelings and impressions at key moments in the novel (such as Alyosha's moment of crisis in Book Seven, or Dmitry's frantic quest for 3,000 rubles in Book Eight). But at other times, he falls back on rumor, or presents conflicting theories about an event or experience.

An early example of this occurs in Book One, Chapter One, when the narrator describes Fyodor's reaction to the death of his first wife, who had abandoned him for a poor seminarian. The narrator reports that Fyodor was drunk when he heard about his wife's demise, and he then offers two conflicting accounts of Fyodor's reaction. Some people say that he ran along the street raising his hands in joy to the heavens, while according to others, he began crying like a little child, so much so that it was pitiful to look at him. The narrator comments: "It is quite possible that both versions were true, that is, that he rejoiced at his release, and at the same time wept for her who released him—both at the same time" (13). In declining to tell the reader what actually occurred, the narrator suggests the existence of fundamental contradictions within Fyodor's soul and indicates that the sources of human motivation may not be entirely clear. Indeed, one of Dmitry Karamazov's most memorable comments is that "man is broad, too broad" (98). Dostoevsky liked to provide his characters with the possibility of acting in unexpected ways. Many of his characters actively resist definition by another; they wish to preserve their autonomy and freedom of action at all costs.

In some cases, however, the narrator provides no direct access into a character's internal thought processes, and in these cases, the character may remain a shadowy, enigmatic figure. The best example of this is Pavel Smerdyakov. Although the reader learns that Smerdyakov was fond of hanging cats and burying them with a mock funeral service, and later overhears Smerdyakov declaring his dislike of Russia, he haunts the novel as a mysterious figure whose deepest motivations are never entirely clear, and it is not difficult for the reader to detect in him (or project onto him) a sinister, demonic aura.

Of course, it is Dostoevsky himself who stands behind the narrator and manipulates these effects of disclosure or revelation. Dostoevsky uses this type of narrator figure to shape the reader's reactions to the novel's characters and events. By allowing the reader to have insight into a character's intimate feelings, Dostoevsky might encourage the reader's empathy for that character. By having the narrator confess ignorance about an event or someone's motivation, Dostoevsky can create some suspense and whet the reader's appetite for further revelation. This occurs in the very first sentence of the novel, when the narrator mentions Fyodor's "tragic and obscure death," which happened thirteen years earlier and "which I shall describe in its proper place" (11). As it turns out, this "proper place" does not arise for several hundred pages. What is more, when the narrator gets to the point where it appears that the murder of Fyodor might actually occur (with Dmitry pulling a brass pestle out of his pocket as he stares with loathing at his father), the narrator suddenly suspends the narration with an ellipsis. In some cases, Dostoevsky's decision to have the narrator make reference to some unexpected, shocking event (as at the end of Book Six, when the narrator says that after Father Zosima's death "something happened" that was "unexpected," "strange," "upsetting," and "bewildering" [280]) can be ascribed to the fact that the novel was being published serially, and it was common for writers of serial novels to stimulate their readers' desire for further installments of the work. Yet this is not always the case in *The Brothers Karamazov*, for many of the serialized books of the novel were intended by Dostoevsky to convey a sense of thematic unity or wholeness.[5] Nonetheless, the author's deployment of hints about future events, as well as the use of recurring theme and imagery, all formed part of his larger concern with the novel's design and structure, as we shall see in the next section.

The Brothers Karamazov is a capacious work, and along with the main narrator one finds a series of secondary and tertiary narrators who report on incidents, tell anecdotes, or provide documentary material to flesh out the main tale. Important secondary narrators include Father Zosima in Book Six, who tells Alyosha and the monks in attendance about his younger years; Ivan Karamazov in Book Five, who narrates for Alyosha a series of stories about horrific child abuse and then delivers an oral account of his famous tale of the Grand Inquisitor; and Grushenka Svetlova in Book Seven, who recounts a simple folk tale about a greedy woman whose single good deed was giving an onion to one less fortunate than herself.

Each of these inserted narratives is related in a distinctive style of its own. According to the narrator, Alyosha wrote down the account of Father Zosima's life from memory, some time after Zosima's life. The account is ostensibly the record of Zosima's last speech to his followers, but the narrator reasonably speculates that Alyosha may have included material he had heard from Zosima on previous occasions. The account itself is characterized as a *zhitie*, a specific genre used to convey the lives of saints in early Orthodox literature. The use of the term *zhitie* signals the holiness of its subject and the fact that this narrative has deep roots in traditional Orthodox literature. Of additional interest, however, is the fact that when the narrator describes Alyosha's own life at the beginning of the novel, he does so in terms that recall the form and content of the traditional saint's life. The reader learns, for example, that Alyosha was fond of going off to a corner to read books, and that he was "seldom playful" (23), yet he was well-liked, generous, and so on. In this way, Alyosha (whose proper name is Alexey, the name of one of the most popular saints in Orthodox Christianity), will be perceived by the reader familiar with the genre of saints' lives as sharing some fundamental characteristics with those holy figures.[6]

The fact that Alyosha has transcribed Father Zosima's life and words carries additional significance in the design of the novel. Dostoevsky allows each of the brothers to deliver his "word" in the opening books of the novel. Dmitry makes his "confession" in Book Three, relying heavily on Schiller's poetry to do so. Ivan articulates his questions about the justice of God's universe in Book Five, and he goes on in that scene to present his original tale of the Grand Inquisitor. Logically, it would next be Alyosha's turn to express his innermost feelings or thoughts, yet he does not immediately do so. Instead, Dostoevsky gives us Alyosha's written narrative about Father Zosima in Book Six. Symbolically, at least, it appears that Alyosha's "word" is that of Father Zosima. Unlike Ivan, whose account of the Grand Inquisitor is an original creation and raises troubling questions about Ivan's true views on humanity, Alyosha does not put himself forward through some bold new literary creation, but rather allows his beloved mentor to speak for him. For the moment, at least, his word is aligned with that of a higher authority.

Ivan's tale of the Grand Inquisitor reveals much about its creator, not only in its content or message, but also in its form. W. J. Leatherbarrow asserts that its "artificiality and lack of truth shine through in its tacky Gothic romanticism, its sentimental and corny imagery, its overblown rhetorical flourishes, and its self-conscious (and inexact) use of quotation" (*Devil's Vaudeville*, 156). Dostoevsky used these stylistic lapses to spur the reader to look upon Ivan's grand creation with some skepticism. A striking contrast to this narrative, however, is formed by Grushenka's tale of the greedy woman and the onion. Like Alyosha, Grushenka does not put forth an original word of her own here. Her reliance on a folk tale reveals her important link to a group of people who have not been corrupted by Western ideas or skepticism. The tale itself offers a simple lesson about the evils of selfishness, yet Grushenka takes from it a message of hope and redemption: one small deed might redeem a life of wrongdoing. And her enthusiasm for this message affects Alyosha as well. Indeed, this simple narrative about the need to overcome one's selfish impulses and to think of others helps Alyosha transcend the baleful influence of Ivan's discourse, with its prominent assertion of ego. Grushenka's brief story, like the other narratives in *The Brothers Karamazov*, contribute to the magnificent interweaving of diverse viewpoints and voices that make this such a distinctive novel.

Patterns of recurrence

One of the techniques that Dostoevsky deployed to add unity and cohesion to his long masterpiece was the use of recurring images, motifs, and plot incidents. In some cases, a specific detail or word recurs at a key moment in the plot, and in other cases, some action or event in one part of the novel might find an echo in a later action or event, a sequence that has been called a "situation rhyme" by the Dutch scholar J. M. Meijer ("Situation Rhyme in a Novel of Dostoevskij"). Perhaps the most prominent of these recurring images is that of the seed or kernel, which makes its appearance as early as the epigraph to the novel: "Verily, verily, I say unto you, except a corn of wheat fall into the ground and die, it abideth alone: but if it die, it bringeth forth much fruit" (Jn 12.24). These words, uttered by Jesus the week before he would be seized and crucified, speak of death and resurrection. Death does not mean the cessation of life. Rather, it is a necessary condition for the flowering of new life. This is one of the central themes of *The Brothers Karamazov*, which deals with the murder of the Karamazov patriarch, the death of Alyosha's beloved mentor Zosima, and the death of the young boy Ilyusha. What is the meaning of these deaths, the novel asks. Can any good come from them?

The specific passage itself recurs twice in the novel. In the first instance, in the opening pages of Book Six, Father Zosima asks Alyosha if he had recently seen his brother Dmitry, for Zosima had detected in Dmitry's eyes an intimation of great suffering in the future. Zosima then utters the words from the Gospel of John, thus intimating that Dmitry's suffering may result in some beneficial consequences. The Gospel passage recurs later in Book Six when Zosima narrates the story of how he advised a man guilty of murder to go and confess his crime. He shows the man the Gospel passage, again with the implication that whatever suffering the man might have to experience could result in positive benefits. As it turns out, Zosima's suggestions seem to find validation in the two men's experience.

The seed imagery, however, has wider resonance in the novel. Dostoevsky uses it in a metaphorical sense to evoke a situation where an idea or emotion that is planted within one's soul early in life can re-emerge later in life with salutary results. Again, it is Zosima who articulates this notion most prominently, and he does so at several points in the homily he delivers to Alyosha and his other followers. He recalls the first time he "consciously received the seed of God's word" in his soul; he was in church, and the story of Job was read aloud (251). He then instructs the priests to read the Bible aloud to the peasantry. In his words, "Only a little tiny seed is needed—drop it into the soul of the peasant and it won't die, it will live in his soul all his life, it will be hidden in the midst of his darkness, in the midst of the stench of his sins, like a bright spot, like a great reminder" (254). At several points in the novel Dostoevsky indicates that a memory of some positive experience can resurface later in life and have a beneficial effect on the one in whom the memory arises.

On the other hand, almost everything in Dostoevsky's fictional world has a dual quality: something that may be positive in one context can be negative in another. The famous expression of the Dmitry's defense attorney—"a knife that cuts both ways" ("palka o dvukh kontsakh"; literally: "a stick with two ends")—is entirely appropriate for much of Dostoevsky's work. As Bakhtin put it: "Everything in his world lives on the very border of its opposite" (*Problems of Dostoevsky's Poetics*, 176). Thus, just as the word of God can abide as a positive influence in one's soul, so too an unkind word may leave a dire impression on the soul of a sensitive person. Zosima warns about the impact of harsh words on impressionable children: "You don't know it, but you may have sown an evil seed in him and it may grow, and all because you were not careful before the child" (275). Because the maltreatment of children is one of the major themes of the novel, Zosima's warning here carries special resonance, and readers will have occasion to recall this when they listen to Ivan's contemptuous remarks about Liza Khokhlakova later in the work. The seed imagery is so pervasive that even Ivan's devil uses it when he reveals that he is trying to spark some elements of faith within Ivan. Characteristically, the devil speaks in ironic tones, and he uses a diminutive suffix on the word "seed," but his perspective on the workings of small influences is not unlike Zosima's: "I shall sow in you only a tiny little seed of faith, and out of it will grow an oak tree—and such an oak tree that, sitting on it, you will long to enter the ranks of the 'desert fathers and chaste women'" (542–3).

Zosima uses seed imagery not only in reference to a potential process of internal maturation and development, he invests it with cosmic resonance when he uses it to suggest a deep connection between our world and worlds existing elsewhere. Stating that much is hidden from humanity, but that we have a secret sense of connection to other, higher realms, Zosima declares: "God took seeds from different worlds and sowed them on this earth, and His garden grew up and everything came up that could come up, but what grows lives and is alive only through the feeling of its contact with other mysterious worlds" (276). Zosima's belief in a hidden reality stands in sharp contrast to Ivan Karamazov's more empirical "Euclidean" world-view.

The seed imagery itself forms only one part of a larger thematic network in the novel dealing with agricultural images and motifs. The very name "Dmitry" derives from "Demeter," the Greek goddess of agriculture and grain. Demeter figures significantly in the novel under her Roman name "Ceres" in one of the poems that Dmitry quotes during his "confession" to Alyosha in Book Three. In the excerpt Dmitry quotes, Schiller paints a vivid picture of a blighted earth: while searching for her missing child Persephone, Ceres has ceased to bless the earth with her fertile powers, and now: "where'er the grieving goddess / Turns her melancholy gaze, / Man in deepest degradation / Ceres beholds everywhere" (97). At this point in the narrative, Dmitry identifies himself with man "in deepest degradation," but later in the novel he will have a dream of a similarly blighted landscape but will move from identification with the one who suffers to a desire to relieve the suffering of others. The suffering that Zosima had foreseen for Dmitry is destined to lead to Dmitry's subsequent regeneration.

A second set of recurring images revolves around the motif of the setting sun. One of Alyosha's earliest and most crucial memories is of his mother weeping profusely and holding him up to an icon of the Mother of God as if to put him under Mary's protection. While the theme of Mary as a protector or intercessor plays a major role in the novel (and is evoked, for example, by Ivan in his introduction to the tale about the Grand Inquisitor), what is noteworthy here is Alyosha's memory of the way the sunlight came into the room: "he remembered one evening, in the summer, quiet, an open window, the slanting rays of the setting sun (those slanting rays he remembered most vividly of all)" (22). The narrator later speculates about whether it was the memory of these slanting rays illuminating the holy icon that led Alyosha to the monastery and Father Zosima (29).

These "slanting rays" will recur twice more in the novel, and in both cases it is Father Zosima who mentions them. In the first instance, Zosima is recalling his interactions with his older brother Markel, who died at a relatively young age. He remembers one evening when his brother called him into his room: "the sun was setting, and it illuminated the entire room with a slanting ray"

(250). Markel looked at him lovingly and then instructed him to go outside, and "play now, live for me" (250). Like Alyosha's memory, this memory is precious to Zosima, and he recalled it "many times" in his life. Later, when he discusses the implications of Job's life-changing experiences, he discusses the effect of the passage of time on the emotions. He then acknowledges that although he blesses the rising sun each day, he loves even more the sunset, with "its long slanting rays" and the quiet, touching memories that accompany it (252). The association between the slanting rays of the setting sun and memory in Zosima's discourse is striking when one considers its importance for Alyosha as well, and one wonders whether these moments had special meaning for Alyosha as he transcribed them. At the very least, they suggest an intimate, and important, link between Alyosha and his beloved mentor.

True to the notion that positive elements in Dostoevsky have their negative equivalents, the setting sun is depicted in quite a different tonality when the fanatic Father Ferapont disrupts the prayers being read over Zosima's body and relishes the fact that the body seems to be decaying at a faster than normal rate. Although he is ordered to leave the cell, he rushes outside and falls to the ground, shouting: "My God has conquered! Christ has conquered with the setting sun!" (290). The tranquility and joy of Zosima's recollections are shattered by the embittered monk's ravings, and this incident adds to Alyosha's momentary despair. Yet although the setting sun may be a harbinger of death, it can also be seen as a sign of the coming sunrise of a new day, and radiant light emanating from the sun also has its place in the novel. After Alyosha's crisis of doubt following the death of Zosima, he has a joyful vision of the monk resurrected, and in his vision, Zosima beckons him to gaze upon "our Sun," that is, the Lord. Here we find an evocation of Christ Pantocrator, the risen Christ depicted in icons as the ruler of the world. The image of the setting sun has evolved into a symbol of resurrection and triumph.

A compelling example of how a small incident in *The Brothers Karamazov* can have a rippling effect over several other episodes arises in the first encounter between Alyosha and the persecuted child Ilyusha Snegiryov in Book Four, Chapter Three. Alyosha notices the boy involved in a rock-throwing altercation with several other boys, and seeing that the boy is fighting by himself against the others, he tries to intervene. When he approaches the boy, the child attempts to rebuff him and then insults him, but when Alyosha doesn't retaliate and begins to walk away, the boy throws the largest stone he has at him. Again, Alyosha refuses to retaliate, and now the boy savagely bites Alyosha's middle finger, clamping down for "ten seconds." Although bleeding and in pain, Alyosha quietly asks the child: "what have I done to you?" and "How have I wronged you?" (158, 159). Alyosha's gentle response astonishes the boy, and he runs away in tears.

This incident has several echoes in the novel. Although it is a rock that seemingly stands between Ilyusha and Alyosha, it is at a rock that Alyosha will deliver the climactic speech in the novel. Standing by the large rock that had had special meaning for Ilyusha and his father (and that served as the location for an important explanation by Captain Snegiryov to Alyosha about Ilyusha's behavior), Alyosha is suddenly inspired to give a speech to the boys who had changed from Ilyusha's antagonists to his dear friends. In the speech Alyosha calls upon the boys to remember Ilyusha, stating that one good memory may keep them from doing some evil in the future, and he affirms for them the future resurrection of the dead and a final reunion of all the boys. Noting that Alyosha's speech is delivered to "about twelve" children, critics have linked Alyosha's position here to that of Christ surrounded by his disciples. In this context, then, it is worth noting that according to the Gospel of Matthew, Jesus said to Simon Peter: "thou art Peter, and on this rock I will build my church" (Mt. 16.18). The rock that signaled division and enmity early in *The Brothers Karamazov* ends up heralding a new union and a joyous future.[7]

The incident of the bitten finger also has significance in the novel's treatment of Liza Khokhlakova. Alyosha goes to the Khokhlakova household immediately after his encounter with Ilyusha and he tells Liza what has occurred. She gives directions to her mother about how to bandage the injured finger. This episode perhaps made a deep impact on her, for later in the novel (Book Eleven, Chapter Three), when she experiences a paroxysm of anger both at the world and at herself, she dismisses Alyosha from her room and then slams the door on her finger. Releasing it after "ten seconds," she stares at the blackening finger and the blood oozing out from behind the fingernail and she whispers: "I am a wretch, wretch, wretch, wretch!" (494). The spirit of anger, resentment, and self-centeredness that has taken possession of Liza contrasts pointedly with the tenderness, compassion, and selflessness that Alyosha had displayed toward Ilyusha.

Liza's act of slamming the door on her finger has added resonance, and it looks back not only to Alyosha's encounter with Ilyusha in Book Four, but also to Father Ferapont's bizarre claim that he once caught the tail of a devil in the door of the Father Superior's room (also in Book Four). As he put it: "I was quick and slammed the door, pinching his tail in it" (150). He subsequently made the sign of the cross over the devil and it died on the spot where it continues to smell. Ferapont's ability to see devils links him further to Liza in her late encounter with Alyosha, for she tells Alyosha of a dream that she has of tempting devils to approach her only to repel them with the sign of the cross. Alyosha, it should be noted, claims (somewhat surprisingly) that he used to have the same dream. Liza's perverse fascination with devils provides an echo of Ferapont's savage spirituality, and it foreshadows the climactic episode of a demonic encounter, Ivan's meeting with the devil toward the end of Book Eleven. As we shall see in our reading of the novel, Ivan is very much implicated in Liza's flirtation with the demonic.

It should now be clear how individual images and events can have multiple associations in Dostoevsky's work. Through this system of linkages and recurrences, Dostoevsky weaves a densely-textured web that encourages multiple readings to explore its richness.

Suggestions for further analysis

There are many images and themes that run through *The Brothers Karamazov*, adding depth and complexity to the work. Readers who trace these themes and images throughout the novel will find their appreciation of the novel greatly enhanced. Two major themes that can be explored in this way are memory and justice. Both Father Zosima in Book Six and Alyosha in the speech he delivers at the end of the novel suggest that the retention of a good memory can play a significant, positive role in a person's life. Dostoevsky provides moments when such positive memories arise in the consciousness of Zosima and Alyosha, but he also includes episodes in which people *forget* something vital, and this forget-fulness leads to troublesome consequences. Fyodor Karamazov, for example, literally "forgot" about his children after the death of their mothers, and this neglect surely contributed to the atmos-phere of alienation from and resentment toward their father that one detects in Dmitry and Ivan. Alyosha too experiences a crucial episode of forgetfulness after the death of Father Zosima: his preoccupation with this death, and with Ivan's anguished protest about the order of God's universe, lead him to forget about his brother Dmitry at moment of crisis in Dmitry's life. This failure to seek out Dmitry may have helped contribute to the situation where Dmitry ends up being charged with his father's murder. Readers can track the development of the broad theme of memory and forgetting over the course of the entire novel.[8]

A second large theme that appears in many forms throughout the novel is justice. Beginning with Fyodor's cynical questions about what kind of justice there can be if there are no hooks in hell to drag him there after death, the novel touches upon the question of justice in numerous ways. Ivan and the monks discuss secular versus religious forms of justice in Zosima's cell; Ivan stridently questions the justice of a universe in which innocent children have to suffer; Alyosha plunges into despair when he considers the injustice of Zosima's body decaying so rapidly after the monk dies; and the culminating event in the novel—the trial of Dmitry Karamazov—results in his conviction for a crime he doesn't commit: a striking model of injustice in human affairs. The quest for justice, and the various forms in which issues of justice and injustice are raised, make a fertile subject for further analysis and discussion.

Notes

1 For a stimulating discussion of the complex, often contradictory elements that are contained within each member of the Karamazov family, see Robert Belknap's comments on "Karamazovism" in *The Structure of the Brothers Karamazov*, 18–26.

2 Carl Gustav Jung called the shadow the "negative" side of the personality: "the sum of all those unpleasant qualities we like to hide." See his *Two Essays on Analytical Psychology*, 66n. 5.

3 For a brief discussion of the stylistic features of Zosima's speech and their intended effect, see Nathan Rosen, "Style and Structure in the *Brothers Karamazov*," 358–60.

4 See Malcolm V. Jones, "Silence in *The Brothers Karamazov*," for a discussion of the types and uses of silence in the novel.

5 In fact, Dostoevsky wrote to Nikolay Lyubimov about his vision for the books of the novel following Book Five: "everything that follows from now on will be in finished form for each book. That is, no matter how small or large the fragment, it will contain something whole and finished" (30 April 1879; *Complete Letters* 5: 79).

6 For a discussion of the affinities between Dostoevsky's treatment of Alyosha and the traditional genre of saints' lives, see Valentina Vetlovskaia, "Alyosha Karamazov and the Hagiographic Hero."

7 Rocks or stones bear another set of associations in the novel, this time relating to the first temptation of Jesus by the devil in the wilderness (when the devil urged Jesus to turn stones into bread to quell His hunger and demonstrate that He was the son of God [Mt. 4.3]). The incident is prominently mentioned by Ivan's Grand Inquisitor in Book Five.

8 Robert Belknap writes about the early encounters with the theme of memory in the novel: "Dostovsky is conditioning his reader to connect memory with love, attention, and family, while forgetting is connected with neglect and debauchery" ("Memory in *The Brothers Karamazov*," 235). See also Diane Oenning Thompson's illuminating discussion of these issues in her book *The Brothers Karamazov and the Poetics of Memory*.

CHAPTER THREE

Reading *The Brothers Karamazov*

Although *The Brothers Karamazov* is a voluminous novel, the work holds together through its focus on the personal dramas of the central characters and it masterful use of recurring images and themes. Harriet Murav finds in the novel an overarching design in which the stories of the three brothers and the structure of the novel mirror each other in a "narrative icon": "The icon consists of three parts: katabasis, or descent into hell; trial; and resurrection, or ascent" (*Holy Foolishness*, 135). As we shall see, patterns of descent followed by potential rebirth or resurrection occur in several forms over the course of the novel. In this reading, we shall analyze some of the key themes and images that recur in the novel: death and resurrection, the suffering of children, the question of divine justice, active love versus passive dreams, the workings of grace, seeds, the setting sun, and so on. We will discover that images and concepts often bear dual meaning: something that may be positive in one context may turn out have negative associations in another. Most notably, Dostoevsky's novel builds in richness as it moves along: ideas and imagery presented in the first half of the novel reappear and reveal their full meaning in the second half. Thus we find that our reading of the novel becomes increasingly enhanced by what we have learned along the way.

The family Karamazov

It is perhaps curious that one of the world's greatest novels begins with one of the most equivocal prefaces from the author in world literature. The author (or, more properly, his fictional representative) begins his introduction by declaring that the hero of his novel is Alexey Fyodorovich Karamazov (Alyosha), but immediately begins to acknowledge that this hero is "vague and undefined" and "odd, even eccentric" (7). Later he states that this is only the first of two novels, and that the main one is still to be written. What is more, this work—the novel we are about to read—is "hardly even a novel," but only "one moment" in his hero's youth (7). Now the author confesses that even one novel might be superfluous "for such a modest and undefined hero," and that he's giving his readers a "perfectly legitimate pretext to abandon the story at the novel's first episode" (8). Here Dostoevsky has taken the device of authorial modesty to such an extreme that he practically invites his readers to close the covers of his novel before they even begin. Yet this odd exposition suggests an important interpretive approach. Dostoevsky affirms that such eccentric figures as Alyosha, seemingly a "particularity and a separate element," may carry within himself "the very heart of the whole" (7). In other words, the reader will be asked to look carefully at individual details and events and find in them pointers to a more meaningful whole. This reader must be an active reader, piecing together scattered elements to form a complete picture. Dostoevsky has included many instances of fragmentation in his novel, beginning of course with the Karamazov family itself.

Dostoevsky devotes the first book of the novel to the history of the Karamazov family. Dissolution, disharmony, abuse—these are the hallmarks of the clan. We note a distinct asymmetry in the structure of Fyodor Karamazov's extended family itself. Fyodor had *two* wives and *three* (legitimate) sons. The proud and romantic first wife bore Fyodor a son, Dmitry, and then abandoned them both. Fyodor, of course, simply "forgot" about Dmitry and pursued a licentious lifestyle. Eventually, he took a second wife, a high-strung woman with whom he had two children, but he did not cease his scandalous behavior, and she died when the youngest, Alyosha, was only in his fourth year. Again, the children were "forgotten." Yet by all accounts, there was still another mother in the mix: according to local rumor, Fyodor took advantage of a feeble-minded homeless woman and she bore him a *fourth* son, Pavel Smerdyakov.

If Fyodor's paternal relationships seem entirely haphazard, however, Dostoevsky himself carefully plotted out the relationships among the father, his wives, and his children. For example, it is not by chance that Dostoevsky makes Ivan and Alyosha full siblings, for it is in the opposition or contrast between Ivan's stance of extreme doubt and Alyosha's pursuit of spiritual fulfilment that the central philosophical and religious tensions in the novel are reflected. As is fitting for the "hero" of a novel, Dostoevsky devotes an entire chapter to Alyosha alone. It has already been noted that Dostoevsky's treatment of the young man's biography resonates with traits found in hagiography, the biography of saints (see Vetlovskaia, "Alyosha Karamazov"). In this chapter we learn that as a child he was "fond of going off to a corner to read" and he was "seldom merry" (23). Yet Dostoevsky was perhaps apprehensive that readers might think that his hero was sickly or somehow mentally challenged (as had been the case with Prince Myshkin, the hero of his novel *The Idiot*), so the writer took pains to stress that his hero was clear-eyed and "radiant with health" (28). Not a mystic but a "lover of humanity," Alyosha has entered the monastery because it struck him as the "ideal way out for his soul struggling from the darkness of worldly wickedness to the light of love" (21).

With this evocation of Alyosha's spiritual journey from darkness to light, Dostoevsky introduces one of the most important image systems in the novel, and he immediately follows this up with the well-known scene of Alyosha's indelible memory of his mother:

he remembered one evening, in the summer, quiet, an open window, the slanting rays of the setting sun (those slanting rays he remembered most vividly of all), an icon in the corner of the room, in front of it a lighted lamp, and in front of the icon, on her knees her sobbing as if in hysterics, with cries and shrieks, his mother, snatching him up in both arms, hugging him close until it hurt and praying for him to the Mother of God, holding him out from her embraces in both arms to the icon as though to put him under the Mother of God's protection…and suddenly a nurse runs in and grabs him from her in terror. That was the picture! (22)

The "picture" that Alyosha has retained as a treasured memory contains several noteworthy elements. At the center is the image of Alyosha's mother holding him, the infant, up to the icon of the Mother of God, seeking intercession for her child. As several commentators have noted, Dostoevsky has created a kind of reflective counterpoint here, with the suffering *earthly* mother kneeling before an icon of the serene *heavenly* mother. Such a reflective structure is characteristic for the novel, as Dostoevsky frequently utilizes the earthly to point toward the heavenly. Just as Alyosha is lifted by his earthly mother toward the heavenly mother, so too do his difficulties with an inadequate or abusive earthly father point to his ultimate striving toward the heavenly counterpart, God the Father. What is more, the scene introduces an important theme into the novel: the concept of a mother's desperate concern for her child. As Liza Knapp has skillfully shown, this theme will be developed through multiple variations in the novel (see her "Mothers and Sons").

At the same time, Dostoevsky also incorporates some ambiguity into this scene that is characteristic of many other episodes in the novel as well: Alyosha's mother is seeking protection for her son, but from whom? From her husband, the boy's father? If so, why does the nurse rush in and snatch Alyosha away from his mother "in terror"? Could Alyosha be in danger from the hysterical mother herself, as Carol Apollonio speculates (*Dostoevsky's Secrets*, 154)? An unresolved contradiction lurks at the heart of this scene, which begins so serenely and ends on a note of such disturbing tension. This complexity or contradiction later surfaces in Alyosha himself.

Acting as a counterpoint to this powerful mother–son inter-action is the scene that caps the chapter devoted to Alyosha: his conversation with his father on the probability of punishment for Fyodor's sins in the afterlife. Fyodor asks Alyosha to pray for "us sinners," thus picking up the important theme of mercy, compassion, and intercession evoked in the earlier icon scene with Alyosha and his mother. He then goes on to speculate on the existence of hooks with which the devils would drag him into hell for his earthly crimes. Now his skepticism takes over, and he states that he's "ready to believe in hell, but without a ceiling," and he concludes: "If there's no ceiling there can be no hooks, and if there are no hooks it all breaks down, which is unlikely again, for then there would be none to drag me down to hell, and if they don't drag me down what justice is there in the world?" (27). In his rambling speech Fyodor touches upon a theme that is of paramount importance in the novel: the issue of divine justice. A cynical materialist, Fyodor casts doubt on the likelihood of justice in the afterlife, thus beginning a line of argument that will be picked up in a much more serious vein by his son Ivan later. (Dostoevsky frequently introduces important themes into his work through the mouths of secondary, sometimes buffoonish, figures.) What is more, Fyodor's mocking assault on the likelihood of divine justice also introduces a secondary issue of importance here: is *punishment* necessary to ensure that *justice* is attained? What role might compassion and forgiveness play in the eternal scheme? Significantly, Alyosha himself remarks with a gentle gaze: "there are no hooks there" (27). These questions will have relevance for Ivan and others in the novel.

The sacred and the profane

Book Two of the novel is set in the monastery where Alyosha serves as a novice for the monk Zosima. Zosima holds the position of an "elder" [*starets*], a monk who, the narrator tells us, takes one's soul and one's will into his soul and his will. Through perfect subordination of one's will to the will of the elder, one ideally finds perfect freedom from the demands of the ego and thus a path to spiritual freedom and peace. If, on the other hand, this system is abused, it may lead to "Satanic pride" (31). Such pride poses a danger for some characters in the novel. Father Zosima, however, is renowned for his kindness, his empathy, and his compassion.

As the action of the novel begins in earnest, Fyodor Karamazov has conceived of the idea of going to Zosima's cell to resolve the dispute between himself and his son Dmitry over the latter's belief that his father has cheated him of his rightful inheritance from his mother. Fyodor, however, does not go to the monastery in a state of pious respect. Hypersensitive to criticism from others, he is ready to take offense, play the fool, and dish out abuse on the slightest pretext. He is accompanied on this visit by Pyotr Miusov, his first wife's cousin. This Miusov fancies himself to be a freethinking liberal, and he is easily moved to self-righteous indignation over Fyodor's scandalous antics. The introduction of Miusov into this scene represents, as Deborah Martinsen has pointed out, a fascinating tactic on Dostoevsky's part (see *Surprised by Shame*, 2–10). The reader, like Miusov, is ready to condemn Fyodor for his outrageous behavior, but Zosima himself reacts quite differently: rather than condemn or judge Fyodor, he tries to bring Fyodor to an understanding of why he behaves as he does. His display of empathy and understanding is meant to serve as a model to the reader who should be wary of turning into a self-righteous judge, as Miusov does. Throughout the novel, Dostoevsky strives to inculcate in the reader an attitude of empathy, understanding, and compassion, and not a propensity to judge and condemn.

During his initial interactions with Zosima, Fyodor is quick to define himself as a way of forestalling definition by others, and two comments he makes are worth pointing out. He labels himself a "buffoon" and asserts: "I don't deny that there may be an unclean spirit in me, not a very high-caliber one, by the way" (41). In referring to the "unclean spirit," Fyodor raises the specter of the demonic here, and this specter forms an important element in the legacy he leaves for his family, particularly in association with Smerdyakov and Ivan. Indeed, just a short time later, Fyodor declares: "Truly I am a lie, and the father of lies!" (44). This assertion echoes Jesus's description of the devil in Jn 8.44: "he is a lie and the father of lies." By making this declaration, Fyodor associates himself with the devil, and he implicates his children in the demonic as well. Of all his sons, Ivan is the most like him, according to Smerdyakov (531), and it is Ivan who will have a face-to-face confrontation with the devil.

At this point, Dostoevsky makes a remarkable move: he interrupts the scene in the cell to follow Zosima outside, where the monk ministers to other visitors, primarily peasants, who have come seeking his solace, advice, and prayer. Zosima's sustained willingness to extend his compassion and love to others stands in sharp contrast to the egoism and selfishness on display in his cell earlier. In a characteristic structure of threes, Zosima ministers to three peasant women, each with a different suffering in her soul. The first woman mourns the death of her son, a child three months shy of three years of age (again one notes the repetition of the number three, which Jacques Catteau has called the "golden number" of the spiral movement of the novel [*Dostoevsky*, 360]). In trying to comfort the woman, Zosima quotes extensively from Biblical scriptures. Unlike many other characters in the novel, Zosima does not try to impose upon other people theories he has invented himself; he is content to allow the words of a higher authority to flow through him to the listener. Diane Thompson comments: "Zosima has so internalized the Word that he sees the whole world in which he lives as an image of that text" (*Poetics of Memory*, 91). After telling the mother that her child is now happy in heaven, Zosima addresses her enduring grief, saying "do not be comforted but weep" (48). Zosima acknowledges the pain the woman is feeling, but tells her also that eventually her sorrow will turn into "quiet joy" and her tears will purify the heart and deliver it from sin (48). This moment is an important one, for one of the major concerns of the novel is the suffering and death of children, with the related question of what meaning or purpose such suffering can have in God's universe. This question, which gnaws most prominently at Ivan's soul in the novel, also had personal relevance for Dostoevsky himself. His own son Alexey died just a few months shy of his third birthday in May 1878, while Dostoevsky was working on *The Brothers Karamazov*, and he chose to name the grieving mother's dead son Alexey as well.

After consoling another mother worried about a distant son from whom she has had no word for a year (a further extension of the absent child theme), Zosima turns to a third woman who, the reader gathers, is suffering from a tormented conscience because she has poisoned or otherwise hastened the death of her cruelly abusive husband. After listening to her private confession, Zosima reassures her that there is no sin on earth that God will not forgive to the truly repentant. Here we have an oblique response to Fyodor's earlier diatribe about the necessity of eternal punishment for one's sins. Zosima asserts that God "loves you with your sin, in your sin" (50), articulating a message of divine love and mercy that recurs repeatedly throughout the novel.

Following his interactions with peasant women "who have faith," as his chapter title puts it, Zosima turns to an aristocratic woman who has "little faith," as the chapter puts it. This last woman, Madame Khokhlakova, is flighty and vain. She alternates between exaggerated expressions of piety and professions of materialist skepticism. In her initial appearance, however, this rather ridiculous figure introduces a question of great significance in the novel: how does one gain (or regain) religious faith in a world that doubts the existence of the eternal? Zosima admits that there's no proof of spiritual reality, although one can be "convinced" of it, and the way this can be achieved is through the exercise of "active love": "Insofar as you advance in love you will grow surer of the reality of God and of the immortality of your soul" (54). This principle is of extraordinary significance in the novel. Reason alone may not lead one to religious faith, but the slow, patient, and steady practice of active love in the face of all obstacles may work wonders.

When Zosima returns to his cell, he finds Ivan Karamazov in a conversation with others about Church–State relationships and the potential treatment of criminals under State jurisdiction and Church jurisdiction. Zosima himself argues against the mechanical punishment of the criminal under the secular legal system. Exile and hard labor "reform no one" and "deter hardly a single criminal" (60). If society were to become wholly integrated into the Church, then reformation of the criminal would be more easily accomplished and the number of crimes itself would be diminished, for the threat of separation from a loving Church would be so disheartening to the criminal that he would hesitate even to commit a crime. Again, Zosima argues for a stance of love and compassion instead of retribution and punishment.

Throughout this entire episode, Dmitry Karamazov has been conspicuously absent. When he arrives, he explains his tardiness by announcing that Smerdyakov had told him the wrong time. This is not the only occasion when Smerdyakov stirs up mischief among the Karamazovs and others. Dmitry arrives in time, however, to hear a further development of Ivan's ideas, now dealing with the notion of loving one's neighbors. According to Miusov, Ivan has asserted that there is no "natural law" causing one to love humanity, and that it is only a belief in immortality that keeps one's baser instincts in check. If one were to destroy this belief in immortality, "nothing then would be immoral, everything would be permitted" (65). Ivan himself now confirms this position, declaring "There is no virtue if there is no immortality" (65). This is an extraordinarily important concept, and it will have tremendous repercussions later in the novel, particularly in its effect on Smerdyakov. Interestingly,

Zosima does not engage Ivan on the validity of his ideas at this moment.[1] Rather, he detects within Ivan's words the anguish of the soul that has generated them. He recognizes that Ivan himself is in a state of profound doubt. He does not have faith that immortality exists, but neither is he certain that it does not exist. It is in this state of uncertainty, Zosima perceives, that Ivan's "great grief" lies. All he can offer Ivan at the moment is a prayer that Ivan's "heart" will attain the answer; Ivan's intellect alone will be of no help here.

The scene in the cell ends when Fyodor and Dmitry become embroiled in a bitter argument over each other's conduct toward a woman they both desire. This is Agrafena Alexandrovna Svetlova, known more familiarly as Grushenka, whom Fyodor labels both as a "seductress" and as "an unapproachable fortress" (67). The introduction of Grushenka into the narrative occasions the first, fragmentary account of Dmitry's public abuse of a retired army captain that will itself have major consequences later in the novel. Dmitry, demonstrating the capacity for sharp swings in his impulses, acknowledges the abuse, but also expresses regret for his conduct. After listening to this rancorous exchange, Zosima suddenly gets up from his seat and makes a low bow before Dmitry. Dmitry, who had bowed to Zosima himself at the outset of the scene, is now stunned by Zosima's gesture and he rushes out of the room. Characteristically, the reader learns only later why this gesture has made such an impression on Dmitry. Dostoevsky heightens the atmosphere of foreboding about Dmitry and coming events.

Soon thereafter, Alyosha and a fellow denizen of the monastery, the venal Mikhail Rakitin, discuss the scene they had both witnessed. Rakitin suspects that the row between father and son portends a murder, and he asks Alyosha whether the thought of a murder had occurred to him as well. Surprisingly, perhaps, Alyosha confesses that he had thought about a potential murder too, but then he adds: "It's not exactly that I thought it [...] but when you began speaking so strangely just now, it seemed to me I had thought of it myself" (73). Here Alyosha seems almost to have picked up some intuition from Rakitin. This will not be the only time that Alyosha demonstrates an uncanny empathy for or connection with the emotional state of another, and it indicates that Alyosha too can be subject to gnawing doubts and anxieties. As he discusses Ivan's state of mind, Alyosha comments that his brother is "haunted by a great, unsolved doubt" and seeks an "answer" to his questions (75). Rakitin now accuses Alyosha of "plagiarism," that is, of repeating Zosima's words. The motif of plagiarism crops up frequently in the novel, and what is important to note is not the fact that one character quotes the words of another, but who the original source is, and in what context those words are repeated. In this case, Alyosha's plagiarism of Zosima's words represents a healthy appreciation of the wisdom of the elder. In other contexts, the process of quotation might carry very different implications.

The sensualists

In Book Three of *The Brothers Karamazov* Dostoevsky leads the reader directly into the heart of the Karamazov family, and the centerpiece of the book is a long, excited disquisition by Dmitry about his passionate impulses and the romantic dilemma he has put himself in. Yet Dostoevsky does not begin the book by focusing on Dmitry. Rather, he leads up to that scene by describing the Karamazov household and its servants, the elderly Grigory Kutuzov and his wife Marfa, who took the Karamazov children in when their father "forgot" to look after them, and the mysterious Pavel Smerdyakov, the child of the homeless woman known as "Stinking Lizaveta" (the Russian word for "stinking" is "smerdiashchaia," and from this word was formed Smerdyakov's surname).[2] Dostoevsky pauses to provide a detailed description of the birth of Pavel Smerdyakov, and his entire description underscores the uncanny singularity of the event.

Lizaveta was known throughout the town as a meek, simple-minded wanderer who would accept alms from the townspeople but immediately put it in the poor box for others. One evening as a group of gentlemen were returning home from their club along a back alleyway, the men spied Lizaveta sleeping among the bushes and began making rude comments about her desirability as a woman. Among them was Fyodor Karamazov, and he alone declared that one could find something attractive about such a woman. Months later, Lizaveta turned out to be pregnant, and suspicion fell on Fyodor, and he did not object when the child she bore was given the patronymic of "Fyodorovich" (son of Fyodor). When it came time for Lizaveta to give birth, she climbed over a tall wall into the Karamazov garden and had her child in the Karamazov bathhouse. Although she did not survive the experience, her child did, and was taken in by Grigory and Marfa, who had recently lost their own newborn, a baby with six fingers whom Grigory called "a dragon" (88). Adding to the eeriness of the episode is the fact that in Russian folklore the bathhouse often appears as a dangerous, mysterious place that was "a favorite haunt of the unclean force" (Ivanits, "Folk Beliefs," 137). The odd circumstances of the child's birth surround him with an aura of the uncanny from his earliest days. As the reader subsequently learns, the child grew up to be aloof and mistrustful. He was fond of hanging cats and burying them "with great ceremony" (111) in a kind of blasphemous funeral mass.

Many readers of the novel view Smerdyakov as innately evil, even demonic. Diane Thompson describes Smerdyakov as "an embodied emanation of the devil" (*Poetics of Memory*, 153), and Edward Wasiolek writes that there is "even some evidence that Smerdyakov and the Devil are one" (*Dostoevsky*, 176). Yet Dostoevsky also provides grounds for a more nuanced evaluation as well. He informs the reader that Grigory gave Smerdyakov "a sound beating" for his activities with the dead cats. Then, calling him a "monster," Grigory tells Smerdyakov: "You're not a human being, you grew from the mildew in the bathhouse." Smerdyakov, the narrator notes, "could never forgive him those words" (111). Given the novel's preoccupation with the suffering of children and the horrors of child abuse, one might do well to consider whether Smerdyakov was truly born evil or whether his troubled upbringing might not have influenced his subsequent development, as Vladimir Golstein has argued in his essay on accidental families and surrogate fathers. In fact, Lee Johnson detects signs of a "deeply spiritual side" within Smerdyakov, and he imagines Smerdyakov engaged in a stunted effort toward "the kingdom of heaven" ("Struggle for Theosis," 76). It is noteworthy, however, that none of the characters around Smerdyakov show him any genuine respect, not even the generally good-hearted Alyosha.[3] Should the reader follow their example, or should the reader adopt a more compassionate attitude even in the face of Smerdyakov's unsavory qualities? Can one regard Smerdyakov as "both evil and innocent" as Anne Hruska advocates ("Sins of Children," 480)? These are the kinds of challenges Dostoevsky's novel poses for its readers.

Having begun the book by showing the reader the disturbing results of Fyodor's unbridled sensuality, Dostoevsky turns to Dmitry, and depicts him in a deep quandary. The interlocutor for Dmitry's "confession" is Alyosha, whom Dmitry calls "an angel on earth" (95). Like many of Dostoevsky's characters, Dmitry is desperate to unburden his soul and to find a sympathetic listener to his saga, and confession plays a major role in *The Brothers Karamazov*.[4] Dmitry's confession takes several forms: poetry, anecdote, and simple dialogue. He begins with poetry, telling Alyosha that he wishes to quote from Friedrich Schiller's ode to joy, "An die Freude."[5] Yet the first poem he quotes from extensively is "The Eleusinian Festival," and the stanzas he cites paint a very different picture than one of joy. Depicting the search of the agricultural goddess Ceres (or Demeter in Greek mythology) for her daughter Proserpine, Schiller's stanzas portray a blighted world, and the excerpt concludes with the lines:

And where'er the grieving goddess
Turns her melancholy gaze,
Man in deepest degradation
Ceres beholds everywhere.[6] (97)

Dmitry's comment on these lines is extremely telling. He states: "There's a terrible amount of suffering for man on earth, a terrible lot of trouble [...] I hardly think of anything but that degraded man [...] I think about that man because I am that man myself" (97). What is significant here is not only Dmitry's concern for the amount of suffering in the world, but his sense of identification with one who suffers. At this point in the novel, Dmitry is extremely self-centered; it is *his* suffering that troubles him most of all. Later, he will discover the possibility of transcending the ego and concerning himself with the suffering of *others*, and with that will come a concomitant striving to help.

At this point, however, Dmitry remains focused on his own feelings, and he now switches from concern with suffering to celebration of the joys of life. He now quotes from Schiller's ode to joy, and once more concludes with lines which he finds personally relevant. Speaking of nature's gifts to creation, the poet writes: "To angels—vision of God's throne, / To insects—sensual lust" (98). Again, Dmitry finds a source of personal identification in these lines, and he declares: "I am that insect, brother [...] All we Karamazovs are such insects" (98). In this very drive toward sensuality, Dmitry finds a powerful duality at work in the human soul. As he puts it:

> Beauty is a terrible and awful thing! [...] Here the two shores of the river meet and all contradictions stand side by side [...] I can't endure the thought that a man of lofty mind and heart begins with the ideal of the Madonna and ends with the ideal of Sodom [...] Yes, man is broad, too broad, indeed. I'd have him narrower [...] The awful thing is that beauty is mysterious as well as terrible. God and the devil are fighting there and the battlefield is the heart of man. (98)

Dmitry is troubled by the contradiction he finds within the human spirit. One may be inspired by the ideal of beauty to strive toward something good and holy, or beauty may serve as a spark for one's baser sensual desires. [7] An essential duality in human potential—either to rise up on a path of rectitude or to dash oneself down in a display of destructive self-assertion—exists as a vital element in Dostoevsky's creative world, and Dmitry stands as a prime representative of this element.

Dmitry now fills Alyosha in on the events that have led him to his current crossroads. While serving in the military and leading a dissolute lifestyle, he became attracted to Katerina Ivanovna Verkhovtseva, the daughter of a military officer serving as the treasurer of the local unit. When the call came one day for the officer to produce the money, he could not do so. As it happened, Dmitry had just received a large sum from his father, so Dmitry summoned the daughter to come to his room alone to collect the money that could save her father's reputation. Despite the terrible risk to her honor and reputation, the young woman did appear in Dmitry's room. As Dmitry now relates to Alyosha, his first idea was "a Karamazov one" (103), that is, to take advantage of her vulnerability. In the end, however, his essential decency won out, and he let her take the money without demanding anything in return. To show her gratitude, Katerina made a deep bow, touching her forehead to the floor. It is perhaps the memory of this bow, a gesture of gratitude toward Dmitry despite the humiliation he had put her through, that came back to Dmitry when Zosima bowed to him in his cell, causing him to flee in shame from the meeting.

The proud Katerina, however, had been stung by feelings of shame ever since that episode, and in a tortured effort to rise above the situation and demonstrate her own virtue, she proposed marriage to Dmitry, seeking to overwhelm him with her devotion and pledging to "save [him] from [him]self" (105). Unfortunately, within this posture of magnanimity lurks a desire to punish and humiliate Dmitry in return for the humiliation Katerina feels he forced upon her (see Wasiolek, "*Aut Caesar*," 89–91). Dostoevsky signals the unhealthy tenor of Katerina's endeavor when he has her exclaim later that she will "become a god to whom he [Dmitry] can pray" (166). Such fantasies of divine status are a sign of dangerous distortion in Dostoevsky's world.

When Katerina first extended her marriage proposal, Dmitry accepted it, and the two were formally betrothed in Moscow. Having returned to his hometown, however, Dmitry fell head over heels in love with Grushenka. Now he finds himself in a dreadful state: betrothed to Katerina Ivanovna, he has used money she had given him to post to Moscow on a drunken spree with Grushenka in the nearby town of Mokroe. He wants to renounce the betrothal, and he is desperate to find the 3,000 rubles he needs to pay Katerina Ivanovna back. This frantic quest for 3,000 rubles sets in motion the chain of events that results in Fyodor Karamazov's murder.

Indeed, the smoldering rivalry between Dmitry and his father bursts into view in one of the final scenes in Book Three. Ivan, Alyosha, and Fyodor are having dinner, and Smerdyakov has launched into a disquisition about the consequences of renouncing one's commitment to Christianity when confronted with the choice of renunciation or death. Smerdyakov takes the position that renunciation of faith is inconsequential, for although one is told that one can move mountains with faith, no one seems to be able to do so, and therefore it is quite reasonable (and pardonable) to have doubts about one's faith. Through this argument, Dostoevsky touches upon an issue that will come to the fore soon in the novel: the question of whether faith proceeds from miracles, or miracles from faith. Smerdyakov takes the position that if one does not witness miracles, one need not have faith. The position that Dostoevsky himself seems to advance in the novel runs in the opposite direction, however: miracles proceed from true faith, and should not be viewed as a means to buy one's allegiance to a religious doctrine. This was one of the temptations presented to Jesus by the devil in the wilderness, and it will resurface in Ivan's story of the Grand Inquisitor in Book Five.

With religion as the subject of dinner conversation, Fyodor interrogates his sons about the existence of God and immortality. Although Alyosha affirms the existence of both God and immortality, Ivan declares that there is no God and that there "is no immortality either" (120). This is highly significant, for if one remembers his earlier proclamation in Zosima's cell ("There is no virtue if there is no immortality" [65]), Ivan has now asserted that there is no immortality and therefore, by implication, there is no virtue. All things are permitted, perhaps even murder.

It is soon after this that Dmitry bursts into the room looking for Grushenka. He savagely attacks his father before running away. Alyosha is understandably distressed by the episode, but Ivan seems strangely complacent: "One viper will devour the other, and serve them both right, too!" (126). Noticing that Alyosha shudders at this, Ivan states that he won't allow to let his father be murdered, but the negative impression lingers. Later, when Alyosha joins Ivan in the courtyard, Alyosha asks Ivan if anyone has the right to look at others and decide who is worthy of living. Ivan indicates that it's perfectly acceptable for one to wish for another's death, and although he once again pledges to defend his father, he somberly concludes: "But in my wishes I reserve myself full latitude in this case" (128). What Ivan is trying to suggest here is that it is all right for one to wish for another's death (even his own father's) as long as one does not actually bring the wish to fruition. Yet as the novel later makes clear, such "wishes" are not harmless, and may have tragic consequences. This is a lesson that Ivan will have to learn at a heavy cost.

The Snegiryov saga

Book Four introduces new characters into the story. One of these is Father Ferapont, an ascetic monk whose zeal for deprivation and condemnation stands in sharp contrast to Zosima's emphasis on active love and compassion. Indeed, even though Zosima is in ill-health and his death very near, he reminds Alyosha of the need to go to see those people who are expecting him, including his father and his brothers. While Alyosha is on his errands, he encounters a group of schoolboys throwing rocks at another child. Alyosha seeks to intervene and finds himself the target of the little boy's wrath. This incident may echo the Gospel episode when Jesus interceded to defend an adulterous woman from stoning (Jn 8.3; see Anne Hruska, "Sins of Children," 483–4). In a powerful scene of compassion and forbearance, Alyosha endures a series of repeated attacks from the child, yet he responds not with anger or retribution, but with patience and a desire to understand. After the boy hits him with a rock, Alyosha asks: "Aren't you ashamed? What have I done to you?" (158). Seeing that Alyosha does not retaliate the boy becomes enraged and bites Alyosha's middle finger to the bone. Yet Alyosha still does not react with anger or violence, and calmly inquires: "I must have done something to you—you wouldn't have hurt me like this for nothing. So what have I done? How have I wronged you, tell me?" (159). At this remarkable display of unexpected selflessness, the boy breaks into tears and runs away.

It is not until later that Alyosha learns that this boy, Ilyusha, is the son of Captain Snegiryov, the man whom Dmitry had publicly abused some days earlier for his role in a scheme Fyodor Karamazov had concocted to ensnare Dmitry with IOUs. Ilyusha had witnessed Dmitry's attack, and he was burning with indignation at the treatment his father had had to put up with. Unlike the Karamazov sons, this child deeply cherishes his father, and desperately wants to defend his honor, not bring him down. Ilyusha was, in the words of his father, "crushed" with his sudden understanding of what "justice" means in this world. Soon, the boys at Ilyusha's school began mocking him, and that strife culminated in the stoning that Alyosha first witnessed and then became involved in. Through this story, it becomes clear to the reader how the circle of abuse can become ever wider unless someone steps in and reacts not with anger or desire for vengeance, but with compassion and a desire to help.

Alyosha goes to the Snegiryov's house with two hundred rubles that Katerina Ivanovna wishes to give the Captain as compensation for Dmitry's attack (she feels him to be a fellow victim of Dmitry's headstrong behavior), and it is at the house that Alyosha learns of Ilyusha's own pain and suffering. Book Four comes to a dramatic conclusion when Snegiryov first accepts the money and begins dreaming of how it can change his family's wretched life, but then, in a sudden turn of events, Snegiryov crumples the notes in his hand and flings them to the ground shouting: "Tell those who sent you that the wisp of tow does not sell his honor, sir [...] What should I say to my boy if I took money from you for our shame?" (183). Here we find a characteristic example of a person who suddenly behaves in the opposite way from what one expects, even though the only person he hurts is himself (and his loved ones). But Snegiryov is afraid that if he accepts Alyosha's money, it will appear to his son that he is being bought off without defending his honor, and he cannot bear the thought of his son's continued disappointment. Fortunately, as Alyosha later explains to Liza Khokhlakova, Snegiryov will eventually allow himself to accept the money: having defended his honor by spurning it when first offered, he can accept it to aid his family with his head held high.

Ivan and Alyosha

As noted in Chapter One of this study, Dostoevsky regarded Book Five as one of the most important portions of his novel. As he wrote to his editor Lyubimov:

> this Book 5 is, in my view, the culminating point of the novel and it has to be finished up with special care. Its idea, as you will see from the text I've sent, is the portrayal of extreme blasphemy and the seed of the idea of destruction of our time in Russia among young people divorced from reality [...] My hero takes up a theme that I *think* irrefutable—the senselessness of the suffering of children—and he derives from it the absurdity of all historical reality. (10 May 1879; *Complete Letters* 5: 83)

What Dostoevsky had in mind here is the extraordinary conversation between Ivan and Alyosha in a tavern. Having depicted the eldest brother Dmitry in the throes of his conflicting passions, Dostoevsky turns his attention to the second son and the intellectual challenge he mounts to the order of God's universe. In both cases, it is Alyosha to whom the main figure speaks, and as the novel progresses it becomes clear that the sensitive Alyosha is deeply affected by his brothers' crises. In this book, Dostoevsky leads up to the seminal encounter between Ivan and Alyosha by following Alyosha first to Madame Khokhlakova's house where Alyosha describes to her daughter Liza his encounter with Snegiryov and offers his analysis of the Captain's refusal of the 200 rubles. When Liza perceptively asks Alyosha whether they are not showing "contempt" for Snegiryov "in analyzing his soul like this, as it were, from above," Alyosha responds: "How can it be contempt when we are all like him, when we are all just the same as he is?" (188). Alyosha here is expressing an important point. Unlike some people (most notably Ivan), Alyosha does not judge others from position of ostensible superiority. He acknowledges his kinship with others and does not regard himself as somehow better or more enlightened.

In fact, Alyosha's recent experiences with the turmoil in his family home perhaps cause him to judge himself more severely than he needs to. He contrasts himself with Snegiryov, saying "I have a sordid soul in many ways," while Snegiryov's soul is full of "fine feeling" (188). Then, when Liza suddenly comes out with the declaration: "I don't like your brother Ivan Fyodorovich" (191), the mere mention of Ivan's name seems to unsettle Alyosha. Stating that his brothers are destroying themselves and labeling this "the earthly force of the Karamazovs," he goes on to say that he too is a Karamazov and he then makes a startling confession: "And perhaps I don't even believe in God" (191). This utterance is entirely unexpected, and it challenges the reader's initial impressions of Alyosha's religious fervor. Alyosha is, however, a Karamazov too, and he is affected with some of the same latent conflicts as his brothers, though perhaps to a lesser degree because of his spiritual orientation. Nevertheless, his admission at this point indicates how deeply the disruption in the Karamazov clan has upset him, and shows that he is vulnerable to an assault by Ivan on his religious confidence.

Leaving Liza's home, Alyosha feels a desperate need to find his brother Dmitry ("the necessity of seeing Dmitry outweighed every-thing" [192]). Although he is concerned that Zosima might die in his absence, he is intent on finding Dmitry so that "I won't have to reproach myself all my life with the thought that I might have saved something and did not, but passed by and hastened home" (192–3).

Ironically, however, it is during his quest to find Dmitry that he becomes sidetracked and ends up in his soul-searing conversation with Ivan, thereby losing complete track of his essential quest. Significantly, the agent behind this detour is Pavel Smerdyakov. Searching for Dmitry, Alyosha encounters Smerdyakov conversing with a young woman and revealing some strongly anti-nationalistic sentiments ("I hate all Russia" [194]; "The Russian people want thrashing" [195]). Of course, such unpatriotic attitudes further mark Smerdyakov as a nefarious figure from Dostoevsky's point of view. Alyosha confronts Smerdyakov and asks where Dmitry might be: "Will brother Dmitry soon be back?" Alyosha inquires.[8] Smerdyakov's answer is noteworthy: "How am I to know about Dmitry Fyodorovich? It's not as if I were his keeper" (196). Many readers will recognize in Smerdyakov's words an echo of Cain's response to God's question about Abel's whereabouts in Genesis 4.9. Having murdered Abel, Cain tries to skirt God's question, saying: "I do not know. Am I my brother's keeper?" Smerdyakov, of course, may very well be Dmitry's half-brother, just like Alyosha, and his denial of responsibility for Dmitry associates him with the first murderer in the human race, a murderer who, according to the *Russian Primary Chronicle*, was inspired by Satan himself.[9] Smerdyakov, of course, does not call Dmitry his "brother" here, but in using the patronymic "Fyodorovich" ("son of Fyodor"), he implicitly invokes their shared parentage. Smerdyakov goes on to tell Alyosha that Ivan sought to invite Dmitry to meet him at a tavern, so it is to that tavern that Alyosha now turns.

The meeting between the brothers forms one of the most important scenes in the entire novel. It is during this meeting that Ivan unleashes his famous attack on the justice of God's universe and narrates his tale about the Grand Inquisitor. This is the "blasphemy" about which Dostoevsky wrote to his editor, and the effect on Alyosha is devastating. Yet the beginning of the conversation offers no hint of its eventual impact. The conversation gets underway with Ivan showing his Karamazov credentials. He speaks of his profound longing for life, for the "sticky little leaves" of spring (199), to paraphrase lines by Pushkin. Alyosha enthusiastically endorses this feeling. As he puts it: "I think everyone should love life above everything in the world." This triggers a meaningful reaction from Ivan: "Love life more than the meaning of it?" It is characteristic of Ivan to be concerned with the "meaning" of life. Despite the instinctual love of life he professes to have, he wants life to make sense to his active, questioning intellect. Alyosha, however, offers an alternative approach: "Certainly, love it, regardless of logic as you say, it must be regardless of logic, and it's only then one will understand the meaning of it" (199). In these words we perhaps find an echo of Zosima's injunction to Madame Khokhlakova to undertake a life of active love, for then she will discover faith. It is through doing and feeling that one attains understanding, not through reasoning.

Briefly the brothers touch upon the subject of Dmitry. To Alyosha's question about what will happen between Dmitry and their father, Ivan gives a startling answer: "What have I to do with it? Am I my brother Dmitry's keeper?" (200). The learned Ivan immediately recognizes that he is paraphrasing Cain's reply to God, but he dismisses the implication: "Well, damn it all, I can't stay here to be their keeper, can I?" (200). What Ivan does not recognize, though, is that he is not only echoing Cain, he is also echoing Smerdyakov. With this secondary level of "plagiarism" Dostoevsky subtly raises the specter that Smerdyakov has some kind of influence over Ivan, or, at the very least, some deep connection.

After these preliminary exchanges, Ivan leads Alyosha into a discussion of "the eternal questions" that Russian boys have talked about for ages. Chief among these looms the "existence of God" (202). Alyosha reminds Ivan that at their father's house Ivan had declared that there is no God, to which Ivan makes a surprising response: "I said that yesterday at dinner at the old man's on purpose to tease you [...] But now I don't have anything against discussing it with you, and I say so very seriously. I want to be friends with you, Alyosha, for I have no friends and want to try it" (202). Ivan's attitude here has aroused considerable debate among the novel's critics. Is he being sincere when he says he wants to make friends with Alyosha? Shortly afterwards he will make an even warmer remark: "My dear little brother, I don't want to corrupt you or to turn you from your stronghold, perhaps I want to be healed by you" and he offers a smile "quite like a little gentle boy" (204). Yet when he goes on to paint for Alyosha excruciating scenes of documented child abuse, he reveals quite a different stance. When Alyosha finally cries out—"Why are you testing me?"—Ivan proclaims: "You are dear to me, I don't want to let you go, and I won't give you up to your Zosima" (211).

The question thus arises: were Ivan's initial expressions of friendship and desire for healing *sincere*, or were they mere ploys to get Alyosha to lower his guard and become more susceptible to Ivan's furious rhetoric? Some critics, such as V. E. Vetlovskaia, have argued that Ivan himself is doing the devil's work here: "Tempting his brother, Ivan is fulfilling a devilish mission" (*Poetika*, 98); "Listening to Ivan, Alyosha is listening to the devil himself" (*Poetika*, 100).[10] Others are not so sure. It might very well be the case that Ivan initially sought to establish a state of friendly intimacy with his younger brother, but as he launched into his series of horrifying anecdotes, he found himself becoming increasingly engaged and enraged, and he ended up trying to compel Alyosha into siding with him in his rebellion against God. As the novel makes abundantly clear, a grave struggle is taking place within Ivan's soul, and the contradictions that surface in his encounter with Alyosha are characteristic of Ivan's portrait in the text.

The launching point for Ivan's discourse is his claim that he "accepts" with his earthly Euclidean mind the existence of God (in much the way the one accepts a mathematical principle) but that paradoxically, he does not accept the world that God has created. The reason for his non-acceptance—his "rebellion"—lies in his awareness of the suffering of children. Much like Madame Khokhlakova, Ivan cannot understand how one can love one's neighbors, although he acknowledges that one might love others "abstractly" and "from a distance" (205). As a consequence, he cannot get terribly worked up over the suffering of adults. Instead, he chooses to restrict his argument to the sufferings of children, even though, as he tells Alyosha, this "reduces the scope of my argument by ten times" and is "less advantageous for me" (205). Here the reader can see how cleverly Ivan constructs his case. Although restricting his argument to children does reduce the sheer *numbers* of people whose sufferings he could enumerate, the fact that he restricts the argument to the suffering of children, and not adults, actually *strengthens* the case, at least on an emotional level. It is far easier to come up with justifications for the suffering of adults than for the suffering of infants. As Ivan himself formulates it, adults "ate the apple and knew good and evil [...] But little children haven't eaten anything and are so far aren't guilty of anything" (205). He continues that if children suffer and are being punished "for their fathers, who ate the apple—that is reasoning from another world, it is incomprehensible to the human heart here on earth" (205). Ivan rejects here the explanation for the suffering of children articulated by such theologians as Augustine with his views on original sin.

Having dismissed the Augustinian explanation, Ivan now presents a series of stories depicting horrific child abuse, first describing atrocities committed by Turks in Bulgaria and then turning to three examples of abuse perpetrated by parents and other adults in Russia. After he recounts the final episode of a child who was killed by a landowner's hunting dogs after he had wounded one of the dogs with a stone, he asks Alyosha if the landowner deserved to be shot "for the satisfaction of our moral feelings" (210). Thoroughly crushed by Ivan's stories, Alyosha murmurs his assent, and Ivan cries out "Bravo" in "ecstasy." It is then that Ivan declares that he does not want to give Alyosha up to Zosima. Ivan's devastating tales of child abuse have begun to have a powerful effect on the sensitive Alyosha.

Ivan winds up his argument with an impassioned tirade reiterating his incomprehension of the rationale for or meaning of children's suffering and then renouncing the very notion of divine harmony ("when everyone suddenly understands what it has all been for" [211]), if this harmony requires unexplained and unexpiated suffering: "It's not worth one little tear of even just that one tormented child who beat herelf on the chest with her little fist and prayed in that stinking outhouse to 'dear God' with her unredeemed tears. It's not worth it, because those tears remain unredeemed. They must be redeemed, or there can be no harmony" (212). At this point, one might suppose that Ivan is calling for the child abuser to be punished; he has already announced: "I need retribution, otherwise I will destroy myself" (211). But now he goes on: "But what do I care about revenge? […] what is hell going to fix here, if these children have already been tormented?" (212). As Ivan sees it, the suffering of a child cannot be redeemed or compensated for by anything, either punishment for the torturer or eternal bliss for the tortured. Even if some wondrous compensation awaits in the afterlife, the fact that the children truly suffered on earth remains.

Having made this crucial affirmation, however, Ivan engineers a curious shift, and his anger pours into a new channel. First, he declares that the mother of an abused child has no right to forgive the one who tortured her child "even if the child himself were to forgive him" (212). Then, he suddenly inserts *himself* into the picture: "I don't want harmony, for the love of humanity I don't want it. I would rather remain with unavenged suffering. I'd rather remain with my unavenged suffering and unquenched indignation, *even if I were wrong*" (212; emphasis in the original). What is particularly striking about this last outburst is its personal nature. (One notes that Ivan uses some form of the pronoun "I" over fifty times in the last two pages of his diatribe.) Suddenly, Ivan's focus on the child's unavenged suffering has shifted to Ivan's *own* unavenged suffering, and he seemingly wants to cling to his own personal indignation over this issue, despite any explanation that might be offered, no matter how well grounded. This abrupt shift into the realm of Ivan's personal sensibilities may lend support to F. Seeley's suggestion that Ivan's particular sensitivity to the suffering of children, especially those under the age of seven ("Chldren, while they are still children, up to seven, for example" [219]), may result from his own childhood experience. Ivan "will not forgive what was done to him (and to his mother?) in the first seven years of his life" (Seeley, "Ivan Karamazov," 133). What is more, Ivan's anger at a God who appears aloof or insensitive to human suffering may draw upon Ivan's personal resentment at his abandonment by his own father. As Michael Holquist puts it: "The filial oppression that sparks rebellion against old Karamazov is transformed into a metaphysical cause for revolt against God" (*Dostoevsky and the Novel*, 183).

By having Ivan shift his focus from the child victim to his own aggrieved sensibilities, Dostoevsky may be trying to whittle away at the foundations of Ivan's arguments. Even so, Ivan's assault on the notion of divine justice through his perception of earthly injustice has drawn widespread attention, and his vivid accounts of child abuse retain their power to the present day.[11] Indeed, one should recall that the writer himself stated that he considered Ivan's argument "irrefutable" (*Complete Letters*, 5: 83).[12] Nevertheless, this does not mean that Dostoevsky abandoned all attempts at providing some response to the issues Ivan raised, and he later wrote in his notebook that "*the whole novel*" was meant to serve as an answer to the denial of God articulated by Ivan (*PSS*, 27:48). Even Ivan leaves an opening for possible rebuttal by insisting that God created the universe according to Euclidean geometry and that he seeks to apprehend the cosmos solely with what he calls "a Euclidean earthly mind" (203) and his "pitiful, earthly, Euclidean understanding" (211). By limiting his conception of the universe in this manner, Ivan tries to turn away from the possibility that the cosmos is more capacious or complex than he chooses to accept with his human faculties. [13] Ivan cannot allow himself to endorse the validity or potential merit of the divine "mystery"—with its possibility of forgiveness and reconciliation in some future time—that will soon be lauded by Zosima in Book Six.

Alyosha himself may sense the limits that Ivan is imposing on his vision of the cosmos when he points out that there exists a Being who can "forgive everything, all *and for all*." "You have forgotten Him," he tells Ivan (213), alluding to Jesus Christ. As it turns out, Ivan has anticipated this objection, and he now presents Alyosha with his "poem" about the Grand Inquisitor. Having attacked the justness of God the Creator, Ivan now launches an assault on the beneficence of God the Son.

The Grand Inquisitor

Ivan's tale about an encounter between the Grand Inquisitor and Jesus Christ in sixteenth-century Spain has intrigued readers since the time of its initial publication, and it has often been excerpted and published apart from the novel. Dostoevsky's vision of the undeniable suffering that accompanies the human capacity to choose between good and evil has provoked responses from a range of commentators, from religious thinkers to political scientists. Yet the full complexity of Dostoevsky's creation can only be grasped when it is read in connection with the text that surrounds it.

In introducing the tale, Ivan compares it to religious "tales and 'verses'" popular in medieval times (214), and he cites one tale in particular: "The Wanderings of the Mother of God through Hell." What is particularly noteworthy about this tale, which Ivan summarizes briefly, is its focus on the mercy and compassion shown to the sinners in hell by Mary, the Mother of God. Mary begs God to have mercy on the sinners, and when God shows her the wounds inflicted upon her own son, Jesus, Mary bids all the saints and angels to add their voices to her call for mercy, with the result that God grants the sinners a period of rest from their torments from Good Friday till Trinity Sunday. Mary's willingness to extend mercy even to those who tortured her child stands in sharp contrast to Ivan's outraged insistence that the mother of a suffering child "does not have the right to forgive the sufferings of her child [...] she dare not forgive the tormenter" (212), and it faintly echoes the scene in which Alyosha's mother frantically sought protection or intercession from an icon of Mary earlier in the novel. It is worth noting that in the apocryphal texts on which Dostoevsky based Ivan's version of the tale, Mary does not beg for mercy "for all [...] without distinction" as Ivan states it; in those texts she intercedes only for Christians, not for Jews. Dostoevsky's (and Ivan's) handling of the tale broadens the principle of mercy enshrined in it. Does the fact that Ivan includes this story as a preface to his own "poem" indicate that he himself feels an inner yearning for the possibility of such mercy in the world? This duality forms a core component of Dostoevsky's portrait of Ivan.

The story proper begins with a short narrative describing how Christ returns to earth during the Spanish Inquisition and performs a miracle by resurrecting a seven-year-old girl who has recently died; Christ is then arrested and imprisoned by the Grand Inquisitor. The bulk of the narrative consists of a long speech the Grand Inquisitor delivers to Christ reproaching him for his return to earth, and outlining the system of control the Church has succeeded in imposing on the believers on earth. Several elements in the Grand Inquisitor's monologue stand out. First, the vision of humanity he evokes is dark and unflattering. He declares that humanity is too frail to bear the burden of the freedom of choice that God has granted to it: humanity, the Inquisitor declares, "is weak and vile" (223). This is a shockingly cynical view of the very people that the Grand Inquisitor claims to care for.[14] Freedom, the precious opportunity to choose at every moment to do the right or the wrong thing, is a fundamental property of the human condition, as Christ would have it. To take away that option, to deprive people of their free choice because of a perception that people are to weak to bear it is itself a form of cruel deprivation.

Second, the Grand Inquisitor reproaches Christ for not having taken advantage of the tools to bind human hearts that were offered to him by the devil during Jesus's forty days of fasting in the wilderness. From the Grand Inquisitor's perspective, the temptations of the devil (whom the Inquisitor calls the "intelligent" or "wise" ["umnyi"] spirit), presented Jesus with three ways to attract and hold human devotion: "miracle, mystery, and authority" (236).[15] In claiming that "man seeks not so much God as the miraculous" (222), the Grand Inquisitor touches upon a subject that had interested Smerdyakov earlier: the notion that miracles are necessary to secure people's faith. This, of course, is a premise that the novel itself tries strenuously to refute. Finally, after mentioning the devil here, the Grand Inquisitor makes a surprising revelation. As he formulates it for Christ: "We are not with Thee, but with *him*—that is our secret!" (223).

Having confessed that the leaders of the Church are secretly following the promptings of the devil, and not Jesus, and that they are doing so for the people's welfare, the Grand Inquisitor presents himself as suffering because of the deception he perpetrates. "And all will be happy, all the millions of beings except the hundred thousand who rule over them. For only we, we who guard the secret, shall be unhappy" (225; cf. also "That deception will be our suffering, for we shall be forced to lie" [220]). With these last words the Grand Inquisitor casts himself in a tragic role, valorizing his own "suffering" for the sake of the gullible masses whom he rules with an iron fist. One might note here that the Grand Inquisitor, like Ivan himself in his earlier discourse on children's suffering, has moved from an ostensible concern with the condition of others to focus on his own emotional state. Significantly, Ivan himself endorses the Grand Inquisitor's self-description: "isn't that suffering, at least for a man like that, who has wasted his whole life in the desert and yet could not shake off his incurable love of humanity? [...] Is not that tragic?" (227). Yet the image the Grand Inquisitor presents is more egocentric than altruistic, more self-serving than tragic. Underneath his mantle of loving concern for other lies a bitter contempt for the herd, and behind his supposed self-sacrifice looms astonishing self-aggrandizement. The Grand Inquisitor's attempt to portray himself as a noble figure reeks of narcissism and stale Romanticism.

It is deeply ironic that Ivan, who began his dialogue with Alyosha with such apparent concern for the suffering of children, should end up expressing such a cynical or negative view of humanity. Gary Saul Morson frankly declares: "Out of compassion he becomes the most profound misanthrope in world literature" ("God of Onions," 110).[16] Perhaps indeed love for humanity in

the abstract may lead to pernicious consequences. Having contemplated the Inquisitor's remarks, the reader might well ask: how
closely should one identify *Ivan* with the Grand Inquisitor and
his view of humanity? The Inquisitor is, of course, Ivan's creation,
and many of the ideas he articulates are representative of Ivan's
worldview as well. D. H. Lawrence famously declared: "If there is
any question: Who is the Grand Inquisitor?—surely we must say
it is Ivan himself" ("Introduction," 6). On the other hand, several
critics believe it important to differentiate between Ivan and his
created Inquisitor. Diane Thompson, for example, argues that "[i]t
is the Inquisitor who categorically rejects Christ and sides with *him*
[the devil], not Ivan, ever" (*Poetics of Memory*, 287).

This separation between the Grand Inquisitor and Ivan may be
detected in the way Ivan has chosen to end his poem. The Grand
Inquisitor had been intent on suppressing Christ's word from the
beginning ("be silent [...] Thou hast no right to add anything to
what Thou hadst said of old"), and he told Christ that he would
have him burned at the stake on the next day (217). Still, after
the Inquisitor had finished his speech, he longed for Christ to
say something, no matter how "bitter and terrible" (228). Yet
Christ simply approached the man and "softly kissed him on his
bloodless aged lips. That was all his answer" (228). In place of
indignation and retribution come love and compassion. Does this
not again suggest that something in Ivan longs for such love and
compassion for himself? We should keep in mind the fact that Ivan
has created not only the cynical Grand Inquisitor, but the loving
Jesus as well.

Although Christ's kiss "glows in his heart," the old man,
according to Ivan, "adheres to his idea" (228). This too indicates a
profound conflict or tension within Ivan, and as Alyosha listens to
Ivan's formulation, he voices his concern about where Ivan stands.
He asks "mournfully": "And you with him, you too?" (228).
Dostoevsky has incorporated a marvelous ambiguity into Alyosha's
question. While the ostensible referent for "him" is the Grand
Inquisitor, the phrase "with him" recalls the Grand Inquisitor's
statement that he is working not with Jesus, but "with *him*," that
is, with the devil (223). As the narrative continues to unfold, Ivan
finds himself increasingly associated with markers of the demonic,
and the question of how willingly he invites this association
becomes ever more important for him and for the reader alike.

Alyosha's meeting with Ivan comes to an end on a poignant note. After Alyosha has asked with genuine anxiety how Ivan can live with "such a hell" in his heart and in his head, Ivan curtly responds: "In the Karamazov way, again" (229). This prompts Alyosha to ask him whether he means "Everything is permitted," recalling Ivan's previously stated theory that without belief in immortality, "everything would be permitted" (65). Ivan seems startled by this reminder of his nihilistic formulation, but he asserts that he will not renounce it, and he asks Alyosha in return: "will you renounce me for that, yes?" (229). Alyosha's response is memorable: he simply gets up, approaches Ivan, and softly kisses him on the lips, just as Jesus had done in Ivan's poem. Ivan is delighted and declares: "That's plagiarism [...] You stole that from my poem" (229). Here again we find a recurrence of the plagiarism theme, but in this instance, Alyosha's gesture may convey disparate meanings to the two brothers. Whereas Ivan's delight may stem from his perception that in mimicking his story Alyosha is, in a sense, validating it or showing approval, for Alyosha, the gesture may mean something else entirely. He is following Jesus's example, showing love and compassion for a suffering man, not endorsing his ideas. Indeed, far from supporting Ivan's premise that Christ—with his divine origins—had too lofty expectations of what humans are capable of, Alyosha shows that he—a human being following the example of the incarnate Christ—is capable of choosing to respond to human suffering with sincere love, not condemnation or suppression. As Maria Nemcová Banerjee observes: Alyosha's *imitatio Christi* "transforms Judas's signal of betrayal into a sign of healing" (*Dostoevsky*, 112).

At this point, the brothers part, with Ivan telling Alyosha: "you go to the right and I to the left" (229). These directions carry symbolic import. The left has often been associated with misfortune or evil (as in "sinister"), and Dostoevsky emphasizes Ivan's leftward orientation here. Thus Alyosha notices that Ivan's "right shoulder looked lower than his left" (230).[17] Alyosha's encounter with Ivan has left the younger brother totally unhinged, and he returns to the monastery almost at a run. But this encounter has had an even more sinister impact. As a result of Ivan's wrenching tales of child abuse, his revolt against God's universe, and his story about the Grand Inquisitor working with the devil, Alyosha has completely forgotten about Dmitry, even though, he would later recall, he had "so firmly resolved to find him and not to give up doing so, even if it meant he would be unable to return to the monastery that night" (230). Whether intentionally or not, Ivan, as Vetlovskaia (*Poetika*, 98) and Thompson (*Poetics of Memory*, 197) have put it, has been doing the devil's work and has deflected Alyosha from his crucial mission. Alyosha's unanticipated forgetfulness will have fatal consequences.

Ivan and Smerdyakov

The encounter that Ivan has with Smerdyakov upon leaving Alyosha forms one of the most enigmatic episodes in the novel. The narrator tells us that when Ivan had first come to town, he had taken a genuine interest in Smerdyakov and had encouraged him to talk to him. Over time, however, he noticed that Smerdyakov seemed to be looking for something beyond philosophical dialogue with Ivan, and had even begun to demonstrate a "peculiar revolting familiarity" toward Ivan, as if there were "some sort of understanding" between them (232). The proud Ivan finds this implied familiarity offensive, and at this moment, as he returns home after speaking with Alyosha, he intends to pass Smerdyakov by without speaking or looking at him. But sensing that Smerdyakov wishes to speak to him, Ivan finds himself stopping before Smerdyakov despite his firm intention of ignoring him. Smerdyakov's left eye winks at Ivan and seems to be saying: "you see that we two intelligent people have something to say to each other" (232). What is noteworthy about this passage is its invocation of the demonic. Not only is it Smerdyakov's *left* eye that winks at Ivan, the phrase "intelligent people" recalls both the epithet that the Grand Inquisitor had used to refer to the devil in Ivan's story and a phrase that Ivan himself had used when describing the Grand Inquisitor's decision to abandon his religious fast and to join "the intelligent people" instead (227). Presumably these people are those who have chosen to follow the devil's promptings. Ivan feels like hurling an insult at Smerdyakov, but to his own "profound astonishment" he finds himself asking an innocuous question about his father instead. Finally, "to his own surprise," he sat down on the bench to talk with Smerdyakov.

How can we account for Ivan's behavior here? In one inter-pretation, Smerdyakov is an authentically demonic being that exerts diabolic authority over Ivan. W. J. Leatherbarrow states that Smerdyakov "seems to have some supernatural and hypnotic power over what hs master does" (*Devil's Vaudeville*, 165). An alternative explanation is that Smerdyakov does not possess any supernatural power, but rather exerts a more subtle influence on Ivan. In this interpretation, Ivan finds something in Smerdyakov that attracts him despite his palpable aversion to the man. That is, there is something within Smerdyakov that beckons to some malign impulses within Ivan. Mikhail Bakhtin provides a masterful reading of the way in which Smerdyakov seems to be responding to the voice of negativity within Ivan (*Problems of Dostoevsky's Poetics*, 258–60).

During the cryptic conversation that takes place by the Karamazov gate, Smerdyakov details a set of circumstances that creates the potential for Fyodor's murder if Ivan were to leave town: Smerdyakov will have an epileptic fit and Grigory and Marfa will take a powerful sleeping potion, thereby leaving the house and Fyodor unguarded, vulnerable to an attack by Dmitry. Suspicious, Ivan asks Smerdyakov if he's actually trying to arrange this scenario, but Smerdyakov denies it. During the entire exchange, Ivan (and the reader too) senses that there is something obscure yet meaningful in Smerdyakov's words, but Ivan does not take the trouble to probe Smerdyakov's insinuations. As Susan Amert interprets it, Ivan is repressing his own dark intuition that by surren-dering to what Smerdyakov has outlined, he is not only opening the possibility of his father's murder, but he may even be encouraging it ("Reader's Responsibility," 111–18). That very night, however, Ivan becomes seized with hatred for everyone from Alyosha to himself, and he finds himself intentionally listening to his father stirring in the house below. This moment of perverse curiosity he would later recall as the "basest action of his life" (239). It would only be much later that Ivan would come to acknowledge his own role in the events leading to the death of his father.

On the next day, although he had previously told Smerdyakov that he was not going to Chermashnya on an errand for this father, he suddenly changes his mind and decides to acquiesce to his father's request. When he gets into the carriage, he tells Smerdyakov this and Smerdyakov answers with a significant look:

"It's a true saying then, that 'it's always interesting speaking with an intelligent man'" (241). Invoking the word "intelligent" again, Smerdyakov seems to be signaling that he and Ivan have come to an understanding and that some bargain has been struck. But just what does this understanding consist of? Does leaving town in the full knowledge that his departure might open the door to his father's murder indicate that Ivan is willing to allow this murder to take place? Or does his departure signal something even stronger and more sinister: that he actually *wants* the murder to occur? Is he tacitly giving instructions to Smerdyakov to make this happen?

Ivan still does not deliberate over these questions at this moment. On the contrary, desperate to wash himself of the entire business, he once again changes his mind and decides to go to Moscow, and he tells himself that he's "done with the old world forever" and is heading to a "new life, new places, and no looking back!" (242). Despite this conscious affirmation, however, Ivan feels not joy, but gloom, and he experiences "such anguish, as he had never known in his life before" (242). He whispers to himself: "I am a scoundrel!" (242). Although Ivan does not delve into his motives for leaving town and the consequences of his action, his emotional state signals his inner unrest. Eventually he will have to confront his conduct and its implications.

The elder Zosima

Having depicted "extreme blasphemy" and "contemporary Russian anarchism" in Book Five (*Complete Letters 5*: 83), Dostoevsky turned to Book Six with the intention of offering a spiritual response to Ivan's caustic critique. Perceiving, though, that it would be difficult, if not impossible, to offer a point by point refutation of Ivan's crushing arguments, Dostoevsky chose to respond to Ivan in multiple ways, from declamatory statements relating directly to Ivan's words, to specific events and incidents whose consequences the reader can compare and contrast with Ivan's own vision of the cosmos. Dostoevsky's first line of rebuttal consists of the biography and exhortations of the Russian monk Zosima. He expressed his hopes for these passages in a letter to his editor Lyubimov:

They're not preaching, but sort of a story, the story of his own life. If I manage it, I'll do a good thing: *I'll force people to recognize* that a pure, ideal Christian is not an abstract matter, but one graphically real, possible, standing right before our eyes, and Christianity is the Russian Land's only refuge from all its evils [...] The whole novel is being written for its sake, but I just hope I manage it, that's what worries me now! (11 June 1879; *Complete Letters* 5: 89)

Partially modeled both on Russian monks and on Bishop Myriel from Victor Hugo's *Les Misérables*,[18] Zosima impresses one not only with his compassion and kindness, but also with his sensitivity to the anxieties and agitations of others. When Alyosha returns to Zosima's cell, one of the very first things Zosima asks him is whether he has been home and seen his brother Dmitry. Although Alyosha had completely forgotten about Dmitry under the influence of Ivan's harangue, Zosima has not. He instructs Alyosha to "[m]ake haste to find him [...] leave everything and make haste" (246). As he explains, he had seen in Dmitry's eyes some terrible suffering lying in store for him, and he hopes that Alyosha's "brotherly face" could help him. He pauses at this moment to cite the Gospel passage that forms the epigraph to Dostoevsky's novel: "Except a corn of wheat fall into the ground and die, it abideth alone; but if it die, it bringeth forth much fruit" (247). This passage, which directly relates to Dmitry's future suffering and his potential regeneration, also may serve as an indirect response to Ivan's questions about the suffering of children: such suffering may have consequences that are not apparent at first glance.

Zosima then continues his commentary about Alyosha's face, disclosing that he sees a resemblance between Alyosha and Zosima's own elder brother, who died when Zosima was young. As he puts it, it seems to him that his brother has "mysteriously" come back to him at the end of his life. By connecting in this way Alyosha and his own brother, Zosima evokes the idea that all people are kindred, and in his linkage of someone who was older than he (his brother) with someone younger (Alyosha), Zosima points to an important aspect of Dostoevsky's religious philosophy—its syncretic sweep. That is, as we shall see, Dostoevsky envisioned a state of Christian grace in which disparate constituents would be conjoined: old and young, male and female.

With this remembrance of his brother, Zosima begins a narrative about his life, and the ensuing chapters of Book Six consist both of Zosima's biography and of a series of instructions he offers on practicing Christianity in Russia. Through this narrative, Dostoevsky provides a model of how one might achieve a state of spiritual resolve and what the guiding principles of such a life could be. Many of the incidents and injunctions in the narrative find significant resonance in the surrounding segments of the novel. One of the noteworthy aspects of the form of this story and the exhortations it contains is that this is ostensibly a compilation by Alyosha Karamazov. The narrator suggests that Alyosha may have recorded Zosima's words and added elements from previous conversations. Unlike Ivan's story of the Grand Inquisitor, Alyosha's "word," if one may call it so, is not primarily his own invention, but rather the transcription of his beloved elder's words. Alyosha does not put himself forward as the creator of a new world order, but as the humble amanuensis for the spiritual teachings of a holy elder (although certain accents may reflect Alyosha's own preoccupations).

Zosima's biography is organized around three main events. The first of these is the death of his older brother Markel. Although Markel had fallen under the influence of a "freethinking" political exile, when he became seriously ill during Lent one year, he underwent a profound inner transformation. Filled with a religious spirit, he began to praise nature joyously and to encourage his family to do the same. What is more, he articulated an idea that would become a central doctrine for Zosima and for the novel as a whole: "believe me, everyone is really responsible to all men for all men and for everything" (250). Zosima himself had uttered this idea at the beginning of Book Four (146), and it will figure significantly in Dmitry's reformation as well.[19] (It also contrasts pointedly with the Grand Inquisitor's stance that it is up to only a chosen few to be responsible for organizing the happiness of others.) Markel's transformation is, in its own way, a kind of Easter miracle, though its full impact on Zosima would not be felt until years later.

Zosima briefly describes his own childhood experiences as a Christian, recalling, for example, how he first received the "seed" of God's word in his heart: a reading from the Book of Job. Job's story, of course, includes both Job's suffering and the death of children, and Zosima's discussion of it provides one form of response to

Ivan's questions about the meaning of children's suffering. Zosima does not try to offer a detailed explanation of the incident, and acknowledges that "it is a mystery," but unlike Ivan, who believes that injustice on earth implies injustice in heaven, Zosima draws the opposite conclusion: "In the face of the earthly truth, the eternal truth is accomplished [...] It's the great mystery of human life that old grief passes gradually into quiet tender joy" (252).[20]

The major turning point in Zosima's life came when he served in the military. Describing his conduct in terms that remind one of Dmitry's time in the military ("Drunkenness, debauchery and devilry were what we almost prided ourselves on" [255]), Zosima tells how he became insanely jealous and angry over another man's successful courtship of a woman he himself coveted. After challenging his rival to a duel, Zosima strikes his servant "with ferocious cruelty" on the eve of the duel. But on the next day, he went out into the garden and suddenly perceived both the extraordinary beauty of nature and the vileness of his treatment of his servant. He remembers Markel at that moment, and especially his dictum "in truth we are each responsible to all for all" (257). The seed planted by Markel years earlier now bears fruit. After begging forgiveness from the servant and throwing his pistol away in the middle of the duel, Zosima announces to his fellow officers that he is resigning his commission and entering a monastery. This sequence of events—striking one's servant and then gaining inspiration for a radical transformation of the spirit—will find reflection in Dmitry's regenerative experience later in the novel.

The third and final major episode takes place while Zosima is waiting to enter the monastery. His own unusual story has piqued the interest of many of inhabitants of his town, and he begins receiving visits from a "mysterious visitor" who eventually makes a shocking confession: he killed a woman years ago, but has never been suspected of the crime. Now, tormented by his crime, and unable to bear the trusting love of his family, he longs to make a public confession. Zosima's patient solicitude finally enables him to take the leap. To his great surprise, however, no one believes him. The townspeople regard him as mentally deranged, and his wife blames Zosima for his condition. Zosima's ministry has begun in earnest: he has stepped up to take responsibility for the travails of another, and he even receives a portion of blame that has passed by the true criminal himself.[21]

The rest of Book Six consists of Zosima's teachings. Although this section has struck some readers as essentially static and out of tune with the dynamic character of the novel in which it is embedded (see Leatherbarrow, *Devil's Vaudeville*, 171–7), it touches upon many of the vital concerns raised earlier in Ivan's encounter with Alyosha. Like Ivan, Zosima staunchly defends the wellbeing of children: "Love children especially, for they too are sinless like the angels [...] Woe to him who offends a child!" (275; cf. also "There must be no more [...] torturing of children" [271]). Yet unlike Ivan, Zosima does not issue a strident call for vengeance. In fact, he argues for something quite different: "If the evildoing of men moves you to indignation and overwhelming distress, even to a desire for vengeance on the evildoers, shun above all things that feeling" (277). What, then, is one to do? Zosima continues: "Go at once and seek suffering for yourself, as though you were yourself guilty of that wrong. Accept that suffering and bear it and your heart will find comfort, and you will understand that you too are guilty, for you might have been a light to the evildoers [...] and you were not a light to them" (277). Zosima's injunction here is extremely important. Rather than standing back and judging others, one should accept responsibility for all people. As Zosima sees it, we are all interconnected, and our own actions (or lack of them) may have consequences we cannot foresee. By accepting suffering, we can both atone for our errors and set an example for others. In a similar vein, Zosima speaks of inaction in a comment that seems directly relevant to Ivan's relationship with Smerdyakov: "If I had been righteous myself, perhaps there would have been no criminal standing before me" (277).

Zosima also comments on pride in terms that are pertinent to Ivan. Speaking of the "pride of Satan," he states that it "is easy to fall into error and to share it, even imagining that we are doing something grand and fine" (276). This could serve as a fitting commentary on the Grand Inquisitor's delusions about his scheme to forge human happiness, and on Ivan's endorsement of that very vision. Pride also comes up in the final section of Zosima's exhortations, which deal with the concept of hell. Implicitly refuting Fyodor Karamazov's pedantically materialist conception of hell (with its hooks and ceiling), Zosima initially defines hell in a way that points to the central drama facing some of the major characters in *The Brothers Karamazov* who experience debilitating isolation from others. Hell is "the suffering of no longer being able to love" (278). Zosima then speaks of beings who "remain proud and fierce even in hell," and who curse the living God who calls them. With his final words, Zosima paints a searing vision: "And they will burn in the fire of their own wrath for ever and yearn for death and annihilation. But they will not attain to death..." (279). This seems to be an unusually dark and pessimistic note on which to end, but the placement of this section on hell at the conclusion of Zosima's discourse may reflect the interior design of some Orthodox churches. As one prepares to exit the church and re-enter the profane world, one passes under or through a representation of the final judgment and the torments of hell, a reminder of the dangers of the world outside.

Yet the book in which these descriptions are contained does not itself end on such a grim note. Zosima, who had urged his listeners to "Kiss the earth and love it with an unceasing, consuming love. Love all men, love everything. Seek that rapture and ecstasy" (278), now sinks down from his chair and bows his face to the ground. As though "in joyful ecstasy, praying and kissing the earth," Zosima "quietly and joyfully gave up his soul to God" (279–80).

Alyosha's crucible of doubt

Aware of Zosima's longstanding reputation for holiness, many of the monks and townspeople expect that some kind of wondrous miracles would accompany his death, and Alyosha is one of those who are caught up in this spirit of anticipation. In a stunning turn of events, however, people soon notice that Zosima's body begins decomposing at an abnormally rapid rate, and the smell of the decomposition causes the monks to open the window of the room in which the body lies. Many of the faithful are shaken, and those who were jealous of Zosima's reputation make no secret of their exultation. Thus Ferapont appears upon the scene, casting out evil spirits and denouncing Zosima's conduct as a monk. Driven away by Zosima's companion Father Paissy, Ferapont leaves the cell, and in a gesture that echoes and distorts Zosima's final movement, falls to the ground "as though someone had cut him down," and screams: "My God has conquered! Christ has conquered with the setting sun!" (290). Here, Zosima's quiet joy and love for all is replaced with frantic exultation and the enjoyment of another's downfall. Moreover, Ferapont's reference to Christ and the setting sun evokes an image of Christ's suffering and crucifixion. The promise of resurrection must await another day, and Alyosha has yet to undergo a stressful trial.

Indeed, the effect of all this on Alyosha is staggering. Adoring Zosima and longing for his goodness to be broadly acknowledged, Alyosha plunges into a deep depression at the unexpected turn of events. Why, indeed, does Dostoevsky subject Zosima to such an indignity? To begin with, this episode drives home the point that one should not seek miracles as a precondition of faith (as Smerdyakov seemed to assert in Book Three). This was a key element in the devil's temptation of Jesus in the wilderness. People such as Madame Khokhlakova are willing to make a lavish show of faith if they can find evidence of a miracle surrounding Zosima's death, but they will just as quickly turn into hardened skeptics when no such miracle is forthcoming. What is more, Dostoevsky intends to put Alyosha through a trial of doubt: this incident serves to temper his soul. But one may still ask, why *does* Zosima's body decay so rapidly? Surely the lack of miracles might be enough to serve Dostoevsky's goals. Carol Flath has speculated that Zosima's body decomposes so quickly because he has spent a lifetime listening to and taking on the sins of others, and now that burden finds expression through the rapid decay of his flesh ("The *Passion* of Dmitrii Karamazov," 599).

Dostoevsky pauses at length on the crisis that now unfolds within Alyosha's soul. Mindful of the error of seeking miracles to acquire faith, the narrator tells the reader that it was "not miracles" that Alyosha needed, but simply "the higher justice": "it was justice, justice, he thirsted for, not simply miracles" (292, 293). This reference to "justice" recalls to the reader Ivan's plaint about divine injustice, and indeed the narrator affirms that "a vague but tormenting and evil impression left by his conversation with his brother Ivan the day before, suddenly revived again now in [Alyosha's] soul" (293). Here we have an example of an evil "seed" that is beginning to bear fruit. Under the influence of Ivan's harsh cynicism and doubt, Alyosha undergoes his own moment of distress. Ivan's influence is confirmed when Alyosha tells Rakitin that he is not "rebelling" against God, but rather: "I simply 'don't accept His world'" (294). Alyosha has stopped "plagiarizing"

Zosima's words to Rakitin (cf. Book Two). He now plagiarizes Ivan.

Rakitin acts much as a Biblical tempter here, offering Alyosha sausage and vodka, both of which Alyosha says he'll accept. Rakitin then tells Alyosha that Ivan has gone off to Moscow, and curiously, "the image of his brother Dmitry rose before his mind" (295). Although this "reminded" Alyosha of something he must not put off, some obligation, that reminder "did not reach his heart" and "was forgotten" (295). Again, the combination of Zosima's death and the lingering effects of Ivan's assault on the divine order has the effect of blocking out Alyosha's crucial mission (which had been reaffirmed to him by Zosima) to find his brother and perhaps save him from suffering. In this state Alyosha succumbs to Rakitin's final temptation: to visit the seductive Grushenka, who has already enthralled Alyosha's father and brother. To Rakitin's amazement, Alyosha agrees to this suggestion as well.

As the reader subsequently learns, Grushenka had promised to pay Rakitin twenty-five rubles to bring Alyosha to her, and Rakitin, like Judas, was willing to betray his friend for the money. Grushenka felt that Alyosha looked down on her, and she longed to bring him under her spell and knock him off his pedestal. The meeting between the two takes an entirely different turn, however. Although she sits on Alyosha's lap while Rakitin gleefully downs champagne, Alyosha's subdued response causes Grushenka to hold back as well, and when Rakitin tells her that Alyosha's beloved elder died that day, Grushenka jumps up, crosses herself, and seems genuinely upset that she had so lightly perched on Alyosha's lap. Grushenka's simple display of compassion has a profound effect on Alyosha. He tells Rakitin that although he came to Grushenka's house looking for a "wicked soul" because he felt evil himself, he has found instead a "true sister" and a "loving heart." To Grushenka he declares: "You've raised my soul from the depths" (302). Although Alyosha had been disappointed that no visible miracle had accompanied Zosima's death, Grushenka's simple act of compassion has the effect of triggering a miraculous regeneration of his soul, and this is not yet the end of the positive consequences of their encounter.

Alyosha's own expression of kindness and appreciation toward Grushenka—calling her his "sister"—touches her in turn, and she exclaims: "though I am bad, I did give away an onion" (303). She now explains this odd statement by narrating the folk tale of a miserly old woman who was condemned to the fires of hell after her death. Distraught by her fate, her guardian angel beseeched God to have mercy on her, and remembers that she once had given an onion from her garden to a beggar woman. God allows the angel to hold the onion out to the woman in hell, and if she can pull herself out, she can move on to Paradise. (One notes that here, as in Ivan's tale of Mary's visit to hell, hell itself can be a site for potential mercy and compassion as well as punishment.) However, when the woman seizes the onion, and begins to be pulled out, other suffering souls see this and try to hold on to the woman to be pulled out as well. Now the woman's essential selfishness comes out and she begins kicking the hangers-on, claiming the onion is hers alone. As a result, the onion breaks, and the woman slips back into the fires of hell. Given one last chance at redemption, the woman cannot overcome her fundamental greed. In telling the story, Grushenka identifies herself with the wicked woman who has done one good deed in her life: she has shown compassion for Alyosha's grief. In Dostoevsky's novel, as if in fulfillment of Zosima's doctrine of active love, one small act of kindness can produce great salutary benefits.[22] As the scene progresses, Alyosha and Grushenka continue to offer mutual expressions of appreciation and care. Dostoevsky's point here is that simple acts of compassion and understanding may be more concrete and effective than the grandiose schemes of Ivan and his Grand Inquisitor.

Most significantly, Grushenka perceives Alyosha to be the first and only person to have taken pity on her, and she confesses: "I've been waiting all my life for someone like you [...] I believed that nasty as I am, someone would really love me, not only with a shameful love!" (307). Here Grushenka gives voice to her innermost desire to transcend the status that people around her have assigned her (and that she has internalized with chagrin and resentment)—that of a fallen woman. She is desperate to clean the slate and begin a new life, and Alyosha's heartfelt expression of appreciation represents an important first step. Alyosha acknowledges his reciprocal gratitude to her by repeating her words to him: "I only gave you an onion, nothing but a tiny little onion, that's all, that's all!" (307).

This event comes at an important juncture in Grushenka's life. She is awaiting a message from a Polish man who seduced and abandoned her five years ago. She is not sure whether she will go crawling back to him or on the contrary, "take a knife." When the summons finally does come, Grushenka departs, uncertain whether she is going to "a new life" or to her death (307). Yet one senses that the effect of the Alyosha–Grushenka encounter will be significant and lasting, and even Raktin seems to acknowledge this when he remarks with bitterness to Alyosha: "So you see the miracles you were looking out for just now have come to pass!" (308). Although Zosima's death was not accompanied by miracles surrounding his corpse, the very fact of his death sent Alyosha to Grushenka's house, where profound miracles of spiritual regeneration have begun to germinate. Alyosha in particular is primed for a momentous revelatory experience.

Returning to Zosima's cell, Alyosha sees the window open and realizes that the smell of decomposition must have become stronger. But he is no longer distressed and he begins to pray. Bone tired, he starts to fall asleep, and in this semi-drowsy state, the words of the Gospel being read over Zosima's body mingle with recent impressions and thoughts in his mind. The ensuing scene represents one of the richest and most evocative scenes in *The Brothers Karamazov*. Dostoevsky declared that this chapter was "the most vital one" in Book Seven, "and perhaps even in the novel" (16 September 1879; *Complete Letters* 5: 160). The Gospel passage depicts Jesus's miracle at the marriage at Cana, and it carries several layers of significance. In the Orthodox Church the passage is read soon after Easter, and it therefore retains association with Christ's resurrection from the dead, an appropriate image for the regeneration that has begun in Grushenka's soul and will now find full expression in Alyosha's experience. Moreover, the ritual of marriage manifests a syncretic principle, uniting the two sexes of man and woman. Such syncretism is evident in the mingling of words and phrases in Alyosha's minds, from the words of the Gospel, to Grushenka's words ("a knife"), to Dmitry's words ("There's no living without joy"). Finally, the Gospel passage depicts Christ's first miracle, and as such, it has the character of an epiphany, or more precisely, a theophany. It is also worth noting that, as Roger Cox has pointed out, Jesus performed the miracle not to "create men's faith" (as the Grand Inquisitor would have it), but to "augment" people's joy (*Between Earth and Heaven*, 204).

As Alyosha slips more deeply into his dream, he sees the room expanding and he sees the figure of Zosima standing up and coming toward him. This image of resurrection has deep significance, for it serves to rebut Ivan's assertion that there is no immortality. Zosima invites Alyosha to join him at the celebration, which as Sven Linnér has pointed out, represents a transformation of the earthly wedding in Cana into the heavenly banquet, with the resurrected Lord as host (*Starets Zosima*, 175). Zosima then asks Alyosha why he is wondering at his presence at this feast and proclaims: "I gave an onion to a beggar, so I, too, am here" (311). The syncretic principle fundamental to Dostoevsky's conception of Christianity is fully manifest here: having the monk Zosima quote Grushenka represents a union of male and female, age and youth, religious and secular life, celibacy and sexuality. After the death of Dostoevsky's first wife in 1864, Dostoevsky wrote in his journal that the highest state of development that one must reach after the appearance of Christ as "the ideal of man in the flesh" is the realization that one must destroy the individual ego and surrender it "to each and to all, undividedly and selflessly."[23] Through this surrender, both the "I" and the "all" are mutually eradicated, but at the same time, they attain the highest goal of their individual development, and this state is embodied in the figure of Jesus Christ: "The synthetic nature of Christ is astonishing." At such a moment, we humans will be "persons who never cease to merge with 'the all.'"[24]

Calling Christ "our Sun," Zosima invites Alyosha to look at Christ, but Alyosha demurs: "I am afraid...I dare not look" (311). As Jostein Børtnes has pointed out, this image of a radiant Christ invokes the iconic image of Christ the Pantocrator ("Polyphony," 409), and the entire scene recalls the Gospel account of the Transfiguration on Mount Tabor (Mt. 17.1–8).[25] The radiance emanating from the Sun here provides a powerful resolution to the image of the setting sun introduced into the novel in its opening pages. As Alyosha's dream comes to an end, he gets up and leaves the cell. His soul is "overflowing with rapture", and as as he gazes at the beauty of the nocturnal sky he suddenly throws himself onto the ground, weeping and watering it with his tears. Clearly this scene is meant to recall Zosima's injunction to kiss the earth and wet it with one's tears (277, 278), and some critics have termed this attention to the earth a "cult of the earth" (Hackel, "Religious Dimension," 144) and "earth worship" (Cassedy, *Dostoevsky's*

Religion, 156), although Rowan Williams rejects the charge, finding the embrace of the earth freighted with broader meaning such as reconciliation and forgiveness (*Dostoevsky*, 170, 225). The entire experience has the effect of fortifying Alyosha's soul. He feels that "something firm and unshakable" had entered into his soul, and "as though some idea had seized the sovereignty of his mind" (312).

Some critics have commented on the vagueness of these formulations and have suggested that its lack of explicit reference to God conveys "little more than nature mysticism" (see Hackel, "Religious Dimension," 164). Yet such critics may be undervaluing the content of the previous scene, with its elements of resurrection, synthesis, and transfiguration, and Joseph Frank suggests that considerations of censorship may have played a role in Dostoevsky's reticence here (*Mantle of the Prophet*, 645). There may be yet another reason for Dostoevsky's use of allusive language here: it might reflect the apophatic tradition in Orthodox spirituality. As Malcolm Jones writes: "This emphasis on the silence of heaven evokes the apophatic strain in Orthodox theology, according to which the essence of God is unknowable and a sense of the presence of God is to be attained only through spiritual tranquility and inner silence" (*Dynamics of Religious Experience*, 22). In any case, the narrator tells us that Alyosha "had fallen on the earth a weak youth, but he rose up a resolute champion" (312). Alyosha's spiritual resurrection validates the Gospel passage that Zosima twice quoted and that serves as the epigraph to the novel: "except a corn of wheat fall into the ground and die, it abideth alone: but if it die, it bringeth forth much fruit." Zosima's death, wrenching as it was for Alyosha, brought him to Grushenka, triggered her compassion, and led to the transformative experience that has now solidified his faith. Now Alyosha is ready to follow his mentor's instructions and leave the protected confines of the monastery.

Dmitry's travails

While Alyosha is experiencing a bracing epiphany, his brother Dmitry undergoes a series of nightmarish incidents. Desperate to acquire 3,000 rubles so that he can repay Katerina Ivanovna and go away with Grushenka with a clear conscience if she gives the command, he approaches several people but meets only with failure. Frantic with fear that Grushenka will choose his father over him, he rushes to his father's house with a brass pestle that he has picked at Grushenka's house. Finding his father alone, he is somewhat reassured, but he now experiences such physical revulsion toward Fyodor that he feels a rising urge to strike him. Dostoevsky leaves the reader in suspense at that very moment, breaking off the narrative with an ellipsis. When he resumes the action, he quotes Mitya saying later: "God was watching over me then" (336), and he follows Mitya running through his father's garden, now pursued by Grigory. For the time being at least, the question of what Mitya had (or had not) done to his father is left unresolved. Reaching the garden wall, Dmitry clambers up, and then lashes out with the pestle at Grigory, who had grabbed him by the leg, shouting "Parricide!" After checking Grigory's condition, and believing him dead, Dmitry returns to Grushenka's house, and learns that she has departed for Mokroe to join her former lover.

Dmitry now decides to go to Mokroe himself, see Grushenka one last time, and then kill himself. Here we see a perverse example of Dmitry's penchant for bold gestures—he will sacrifice himself, or "step aside" (339) for Grushenka's happiness, heedless of the impact this may have on his family and others. He purchases a large supply of food and wine to stage an elaborate feast at Mokroe before his death. Suddenly he is in possession of a sizable amount of money, the source of which is not immediately disclosed. Mystery piles upon mystery, and it is not until later in the novel that Dostoevsky solves the riddles he poses here. Once at Mokroe, Dmitry discovers to his delight that Grushenka has become disenchanted with her former lover; she now declares her love for him instead. Dmitry is both thrilled by this turn of events and stricken with sorrow at the thought that he had killed Grigory. He prays: "Oh, God! restore to life the man I knocked down at the fence! Let this fearful cup pass from me!" (372). Dmitry's words here resonate with Jesus's prayer in the garden of Gethsemane on the night of his arrest. Yet Dmitry is not quite ready to adopt the second part of Jesus's prayer: "if this cannot pass until I drink it, Thy will be done" (Mt. 26.42). His spiritual regeneration has yet to ripen.

As Dmitry and Grushenka declare their love for each other and pledge their determination to begin new lives, police officers and prosecutors arrive at the Mokroe inn and place Dmitry under arrest. Dmitry immediately assumes that it the attack on Grigory that has brought the authorities, and he is stunned to learn that they are accusing him of the murder of his father. He immediately denies any responsibility: "I'm not guilty of my father's blood...I meant to kill him. But I'm not guilty" (388). The interrogation that follows is deeply humiliating for Dmitry. He is forced to take off his clothing and surrender them as evidence, and he feels intense shame when he reveals the source of the money he had brought to Mokroe (he had been keeping in reserve half of the 3,000 rubles Katerina had given him to send to Moscow). Yet when he hears the news that Grigory did not die from Dmitry's blow, and will recover, Dmitry takes heart, and he cries out: "Lord, I thank Thee for the miracle Thou has wrought for me, a sinner and evildoer" (390). Dmitry feels himself to be the recipient of an unexpected "miracle," and this prepares the way for an internal transformation. Acknowledging Grigory's care for him during his childhood, he states that the servant had become "my own father" (390). Thus, Dmitry managed to avoid parricide both with his surrogate father Grigory and with his biological father Fyodor. In the face of extreme skepticism from his interrogators, Dmitry denies killing Fyodor: "Whether it was someone's tears, or my mother prayed to God, or a good angel kissed me at that instant, I don't know. But the devil was conquered" (400). These images—tears, a mother's prayers, an angel's kiss, the conquering of the devil—all resonate with multiple episodes in the novel and serve to mark the importance of Dmitry's sense of his salvation from catastrophe.

Exhausted by a night of high stress, Dmitry takes a short nap, and he experiences a transformative dream. He sees a peasant village that has suffered a devastating fire, and he notes in particular a tall, bony woman carrying a little baby who is crying.[26] In the dream, Dmitry asks: "But why is it weeping?" and then "why are people poor, why is the babe poor, why is the steppe barren [...] why don't they feed the babe?" (428). Dmitry's broad questions recall Ivan's existential questions about the meaning of suffering in the cosmos. Yet as the narrative continues, Dmitry moves beyond the posing of questions. Indeed, he feels "that a passion of pity, such as he had never known before, was rising in his heart, and he wanted to cry, that he wanted to do something for them all, so that the babe should weep no more [...] and he wanted to do it at once, at once, regardless of all obstacles, with all the Karamazov recklessness" (428). Now hearing Grushenka's voice, Dmitry "struggled forward towards the light [...] towards the new, beckoning light, and to hasten, hasten, now, at once!" (428). When he awakens, he declares: "I've had a good dream, gentlemen," and his face seems lit up with joy (429).

Dmitry's dream experience has clear parallels with Alyosha's epiphanic experience earlier, and Dostoevsky himself mentions the connection in his notebooks (*Notebooks*, 170). In both cases, the central figure is plunged into despair by the death (or apparent death) of a surrogate father figure. Then, the grieving man comes into contact with a sensitive woman, Grushenka (it should be noted that her surname "Svetlova" contains the Russian word for light—"svet"). The death of the surrogate father is annulled in each case, by resurrection in Alyosha's dream and by the fact that the wound was not a fatal one in the case of Dmitry's experience. Both men have a dream vision that has a transformative effect on their souls, and when they awaken they feel themselves renewed and regenerated.[27]

Yet there is also a meaningful difference between the two experiences, and the difference corresponds to something essential in the characters of the two men. The spiritually oriented Alyosha has an epiphanic experience that operates on a higher spiritual (and even mystical) plane than Dmitry's more corporeal or sensual experience. While Alyosha envisons a feast at Cana of Galilee and finds himself in the company of Christ Pantocrator, Dmitry sees a Russian village populated by eminently mortal figures. Then too, while Alyosha feels a heightened connection to the solemn mysteries of the cosmos, Dmitry comes away from his vision with a straightforward determination to do something to relieve the suffering of others. As several scholars have pointed out, Dostoevsky's religious orientation centered on action to be taken in this world,[28] and Zosima himself counseled "active love" as an antidote to a crisis of faith (see page 54).

One of the most striking features about Dmitry's vision is the shift one can observe between his attitude toward a scene of suffering and degradation evoked in the Schiller poem he quoted in Book Three and his attitude toward a similar scene here. Whereas at that earlier moment he identified primarily with the one who suffers ("I am that man myself" [97]), here he sees a suffering child and he wants to help, to make a difference, and not merely to experience a passive identification. We might also contrast Dmitry's determination to *do* something about the suffering child with Ivan's attitude of indignation over child abuse that seemed to promise little in the way of alleviating the suffering itself. As R. Maurice Barineau points out, "Ivan can certainly think compassionately; he just cannot act compassionately" ("Triumph of Ethics," 380).

When it is time for Dmitry to be taken away, he fully accepts what has befallen him. Proclaiming himself "the lowest viper," he asserts: "Never, never should I have risen of myself! [...] I want to suffer and by suffering I shall be purified" (429). Stating again that he did not kill his father, he now makes a crucial acknowledgment: "I accept my punishment, not because I killed him, but because I meant to kill him, and perhaps I really might have killed him" (429). Dmitry seems to have arrived on his own at an understanding and acceptance of one of Zosima's key injunctions for those who are moved to indignation at the evildoing of others: "Go at once and seek suffering for yourself, as though you were yourself guilty of that wrong. Accept that suffering and bear it and your heart will find comfort, and you will understand that you too are guilty, for you might have been a light to the evildoers" (277). Now Dmitry is prepared to perform an authentic sacrifice—accepting punishment for a crime he did not commit—not as a demonstration of egocentric self-display, but as an act of Christ-like humility.

Alyosha and the boys

After the tension and high drama of the events leading up to Dmitry's arrest, Dostoevsky takes a break from from the travails of the Karamazov family and turns his attention to the younger generation, focusing now on Alyosha's budding influence on the children of his town. Dostoevsky introduces a new character, a charismatic adolescent named Kolya Krasotkin. Bold and self-assured, Kolya has the makings of a true leader, but at the same time his vanity makes him insensitive to the sufferings of others occasionally. This is evident in his relationship with Ilyusha Snegiryov. When Ilyusha first entered Kolya's school, the other children picked on Ilyusha, but Kolya defended him, and soon Ilyusha "became slavishly devoted" to him, as if he "were God" (450). Later, though, Kolya noticed Ilyusha rebelling against him, so Kolya tried to train him and "make a man of him" by becoming cold to the younger boy. In Kolya's plans for Ilyusha one detects echoes of the Grand Inquisitor's scheme for exercising authority over the masses, and in Kolya's phrase, "to make a man" ("sozdat' cheloveka"—literally, to "create" a man), one recognizes the words used to describe God's creation of the first human (Gen. 1.27).[29] Kolya, in other words, arrogates to himself the power of a would-be God.

As a result of Kolya's coldness, Ilyusha withdraws, and he allows himself to fall under the baneful influence of Smerdyakov. Smerdyakov suggests to Ilyusha that he put a pin in a lump of bread and feed it to a dog. When Ilyusha does so, the dog howls in pain and runs away. As in the temptation of Jesus by the devil to which the Grand Inquisitor referred in Book Five, bread proves to be a substance leading one into the realm of evil. Ilyusha is tormented with remorse, and when Kolya shows renewed coldness toward him, he becomes even more disconsolate and rebellious. Ilyusha's rift with Kolya then spreads to the other boys, leading to the stoning scene observed earlier. In this episode one can see clearly the consequences of a vengeful attitude toward wrongdoing: punishment only hardens the heart of the transgressor and paves the way for further abuse, and sadly, it is children themselves who perpetuate the cycle of abuse.

Once the compassionate Alyosha becomes involved, however, relations between Ilyusha and the other boys improve. They begin visiting the ailing child, and only Kolya remains aloof. At last, he too deigns to pay Ilyusha a visit, and he brings with him a stray dog he has found and trained. Although he has told the other boys that the dog Ilyusha injured must have died long ago, in truth he has found that very dog and has only been waiting to teach the dog tricks so as to impress everyone when he finally appears. Pouring cold water on Ilyusha's hopes until the very last minute, he eventually reveals the dog, and this apparent resurrection of the animal believed to be dead triggers a near fatal shock in the conscience-stricken Ilyusha. In effect, Kolya has engineered a pseudo-miracle to enhance his own reputation, and Dostoevsky underscores the falseness of this "miracle" by having Kolya make the dog play dead, with only Kolya's word having the power to raise him up. Nonetheless, the "risen" Zhuchka provides Ilyusha with a tangible sign that his sin can be redeemed, his guilt relieved. Unfortunately, the means of

Ilyusha's relief has been needlessly (and dangerously) delayed by Kolya's desire to stun and impress others. Alyosha takes the opportunity to engage Kolya in a heartfelt conversation, and it becomes clear that Kolya, whose father died when Kolya was an infant, may have need of a strong father figure: he has fallen under the influence of the radical materialists such as Rakitin. Yet Alyosha's attitude of gentle understanding is far from the authoritative posturing of a Grand Inquisitor; on the contrary, he wins Kolya's admiration with his compassion and empathy.

Book Ten ends on a note of high pathos. A visit to Ilyusha by a distinguished physician makes it clear that Ilyusha's condition is incurable. Sensing this, Ilyusha selflessly exhorts his father to get himself a new boy after Ilyusha's death and to love the new boy instead. Here we find an echo of the theme of children's deaths and the grief of the surviving parents that came up in Zosima's ministry to the peasant women and in his mention of the Book of Job. Captain Snegiryov's own grief is too raw and too fresh for any consolation to be possible at this time.

Ivan Karamazov and his demons

Both Alyosha and Dmitry have undergone extreme crises of the spirit; now it is Ivan's turn. This brother, who perhaps has the strongest intellectual defenses against an internal crisis, resists mightily, but he too succumbs. Unfortunately for him, however, his experience results in a very different outcome. It is noteworthy that Dostoevsky prepares the way for the reader's exposure to Ivan's great crisis by showing the effects he's had on other characters during the two months that have elapsed since the day of Fyodor's murder and the eve of Dmitry's trial.

The first person Dostoevsky focuses on is Liza Khokhlakova. Alyosha is surprised to learn from Liza's mother that Ivan has visited the girl, and apparently, has triggered some kind of emotional distress within her. One day she exclaims "I hate Ivan Fydorovich", and the next she slaps her servant in the face. Hitting one's servant preceded spiritual transformations in Żosima and Dmitry. Here, however, there is little indication that such a transformation within Liza is imminent. When Alyosha goes to meet with the girl (in a chapter ominously entitled "A Little Demon"), he is shocked to see how ill she looks. But even more shocking are her words. She declares: "I should like someone to torture me, marry me and then torture me, deceive me and go away. I don't want to be happy" (490). What is more, she extends her unhappiness into anger at the wider world: "I keep wanting to set fire to the house"; "Ah, how good it would be if everything were destroyed" (490, 491). This is a profoundly unhappy child who does not know how to cope with the distress coursing through her system; it leaves her devastated. She tells Alyosha that she has a "funny dream" in which she sees devils in her room and then engages in a process of drawing them to her by reviling God, and then repelling them by crossing herself. Such a dream vividly conveys the condition of a soul on the brink, drawn to destruction, yet still clinging to the hope of rescue. Significantly, Alyosha does not recoil in dismay over Liza's vision. On the contrary, he confesses that he's had the same dream too. We do not know when Alyosha had such dreams; presumably it occurred before his epiphanic experience. Nevertheless, he demonstrates once again his essential humanity. He is ever responsive to the pain of another.

Alyosha's empathy momentarily soothes Liza, but she goes on to reveal additional torments. Stating that she read a newspaper account of a Jew who crucified a child of four (a version of the infamous "blood libel"[30]), she tells Alyosha that she although she "shook with sobs all night" after reading about the incident, she sometimes imagines that it was she who crucified the child and that she would sit and watch the suffering child and eat pineapple compote the entire time. This is an extraordinarily disturbing image, particularly in a novel that is so deeply concerned with the suffering of children. Liza's perverse fascination with the crucifixion of a child links her with another figure who actually carried out the profanation of sacred rituals—Smerdyakov—and it underscores the spiritual peril she is in. Given the novel's concern with suffering children, it is highly significant that Liza sent for "a certain person" (i.e. Ivan) and told him about the child and the compote. After she tells him that this was "good," he "laughed and said it really was good" (493), and then he left. We should observe that Ivan, who earlier expressed such heartfelt concern over the suffering of children, does not take the opportunity either to express dismay over the fantasy, or more importantly, to try to help the anguished child who seeks his counsel about this horrifying vision. The reader is not explicitly told why Liza had summoned Ivan in the first place,[31] but it is clear that behind her desire to impress him lie a deep insecurity and a desperate need for approval and respect. Ivan's quick departure makes Liza wonder if he "despises" her, and she feels worse than ever: "I shall kill myself, because I loathe everything!" (493). Alyosha is her sole hope, and she calls out for him to "save" her, but she also sends him away to help Dmitry. Shaken, Alyosha leaves the child behind, and Liza, left alone, slams the door on her finger. Watching the blood ooze out from under the nail, she denounces herself: "I am a wretch, wretch, wretch, wretch!" (494).[32]

Liza's association with the demonic (in the chapter title and in her conduct) both looks back to the crazed Father Ferapont (who saw devils, and caught the tail of one in a monastery door) and looks forward to Ivan, who will talk with a devil at the end of this book. She has clearly fallen under the shadow of Ivan's extreme negativity, and it is not clear how her spirits will be revived.

Dostoevsky now turns to another character who has been affected by Ivan's penumbra of negativity—Dmitry. While in prison awaiting trial, Dmitry has been visited by Rakitin, whom Diane Thompson calls "a shallow emissary from Ivan's ideological sphere" (*Poetics of Memory*, 251). Rakitin has been dunning Dmitry with the latest discoveries of scientific materialism. Although Dmitry finds science "magnificent," he exclaims that he is "sorry to lose God!" (497). Dmitry resists Rakitin's theories, and, showing the effects of Ivan's ruminations on immortality and virtue, he asks Rakitin what will become of people in the absence of God and immortal life: "All things are permitted then, they can do what they like?" Rakitin's response echoes both Smerdyakov and the language of the legend of the Grand Inquisitor: "Don't you know? [...] an intelligent man can do what he likes" (497). Despite this onslaught, Dmitry clings to the revelation he had during his dream at Mokroe. Affirming that he has found in himself "a new man," Dmitry declares: "It's for the babe I'm going. Because we are all responsible for all [...] I didn't kill father, but I've got to go. I accept it" (499). The image of the babe is familiar from Dmitry's dream, but it is noteworthy that Dmitry has also embraced the concept of universal responsibility. This was Zosima's idea, which he in turn had received from his brother Markel. We have no clear evidence that Dmitry has heard Zosima utter this, and thus the impression arises that Dmitry has come to this revelation on its own. The doctrine thus takes on the stature of a universal truth, accessible to all whose souls are open to it.

Set in opposition to this, however, is a new issue that troubles Dmitry. If Dmitry is convicted of the murder, Ivan wants to arrange for Dmitry to escape, and perhaps flee to America. As Dmitry puts it: "He doesn't ask me, but orders me" to escape (503). Dmitry is considering this, but he wonders whether such an escape would mean that he is running away from the suffering that he has chosen as a path to salvation. Why, the reader might ask, is Ivan so keen on Dmitry's escape? If Dmitry is innocent, then perhaps he shouldn't have to suffer, one might argue. But Ivan's rationale is undoubtedly more complex. As we shall see, he has been tormenting himself with the question of his own responsibility for his father's murder, and if Dmitry goes off to Siberia to be punished for the deed while Ivan remains free, Ivan's conscience would continue to chafe.

The issue of Ivan's concern about his own culpability surfaces in the very next chapter. Meeting Ivan at Katerina Ivanovna's house, Alyosha follows him onto the street, where he gives Ivan a note that Liza had given him to deliver to Ivan. Ivan exclaims with a malicious laugh: "Ah, from that little demon!" and he rips the note into pieces and throws it away. Ivan then states with contempt that Liza is "not sixteen yet [...] and already offering herself" (506). Alyosha erupts with a pained reproach: "How can you, Ivan, how can you? [...] She is a child; you are insulting a child!" To this, Ivan replies with chilling reserve: "If she is a child I am not her nurse" (506). Here one finds a recognizable variant of those earlier echoes of Cain's words about his brother Abel ("I am not my brother's keeper"), but what makes Ivan's comment so harsh in this scene is his dismissive attitude toward a *child*. Granted, Liza may no longer be seven years old, but she is a child nonetheless, and Ivan's refusal to engage or help her puts the final cap on the series of subtle ways in which Dostoevsky has been undermining Ivan's position of authority on the issue of child abuse.

From this, the subject turns to the question of Fyodor Karamazov's murderer. Alyosha warmly defends Dmitry's innocence, and this triggers a pointed question from Ivan: "Who is the murderer then, according to you?" (507). Alyosha's answer is striking. Instead of simply replying "Smerdyakov," whom Alyosha believes to be the actual murderer, Alyosha responds: "You yourself know who."

Ivan asks him to clarify, even mentioning Smerdyakov, but Alyosha again dodges the chance to name Smerdyakov, and merely repeats: "You yourself know who." Now Ivan is nearly frantic: "Who? Who?" he asks. And Alyosha responds: "I only know one thing [...] *it was not you* who killed father" (507).

This interchange between the two brothers is remarkably subtle and suggestive. In declaring that it was not Ivan who killed Fyodor, Alyosha seems to be addressing what might be called Ivan's "inner voice"—the voice of his conscience, full of accusation and self-doubt. As Alyosha himself goes on to say, Ivan has told himself several times that he was the murderer. Yet although Alyosha is trying to reassure Ivan and persuade him of his own innocence (and he states that it is God who sent him to tell Ivan this), Ivan may hear something quite different in Alyosha's words. When Alyosha does not name Smerdyakov, but only says "you yourself know who," Ivan may hear stress on the words "you yourself" and internalize them as meaning: "look within yourself; you and your conscience know who's responsible." Rather than reassuring Ivan, Alyosha's words may have the effect of spurring Ivan to discover once and for all what his responsibility for his father's murder truly is.[33] Indeed, it is after Alyosha's well-intentioned attempt to console Ivan that Ivan turns on him coldly and declares that he's breaking off all relations with Alyosha and then sets off to visit Smerdyakov to settle this question for good.

Smerdyakov and Ivan's devil

This is the third visit Ivan has made to Smerdyakov after Fyodor's murder. With each visit, Smerdyakov implicates Ivan more deeply in the arrangement and execution of Fyodor's murder. During the first visit, Smerdyakov decodes the cryptic conversation at the gate to the Karamazov house and indicates his understanding that the very fact that Ivan left town after being told what might happen if he were to do so suggested that Ivan *knew* what would happen and was just trying to "get out of misfortune's way" (511). In other words, by leaving town, Ivan was opening the door for the possibility (and probability) of his father's murder. Smerdyakov maintains, however, that it was not he, Smerdyakov, who committed the murder, but Dmitry, and Ivan feels some relief because of this.

During the second meeting, however, Smerdyakov's insinuations about Ivan's involvement become more pointed. Not only did Ivan's departure signify that he was willing to leave Fyodor to his fate, but Smerdyakov now states that during the conversation at the gate he was trying to find whether Ivan *wanted* his father to be murdered or not. He states that he thought that Ivan too, like Dmitry, "was very desirous" of his father's death and so he sought to "sound [him] out" at the gate on that very point (517). Ivan becomes indignant at this accusation, and he strikes Smerdyakov (recalling Zosima's violence against his servant on the eve of his revelation, and Dmitry's violence against Grigory before his revelatory dream; here however, there is no positive transformation in the offing). Now he accuses Smerdyakov of committing the murder, but Smerdyakov denies it. Nonetheless, his insinuations continue: "if you had a foreboding about me and yet went away, you as good as said to me, 'You can murder my parent, I won't hinder you!'" (518). Ivan leaves this meeting lacerating himself with self-accusations, but when he tells Katerina Ivanovna about this, she shows him a letter that Dmitry had written her when he was drunk, pledging to murder his father if he could not obtain the 3,000 rubles he owed her. This temporarily sets Ivan's mind at ease, yet Alyosha's words about his innocence then reopen the wounds, and he goes to visit Smerdyakov one more time.

On this occasion he finds Smerdyakov quite ill, and not at all pleased to see him. Smerdyakov tries to get rid of Ivan by saying "*you* did not murder him," but this formulation only brings back Alyosha's words, leading Ivan to demand that Smerdyakov tell him everything. Now Smerdyakov responds "with insane hatred": "Well, it was you who murdered him, if that's it" (524). He goes even further: "*You* murdered him; you are the real murderer, I was only your instrument, your faithful servant Licharda, and it was following your words I did it" (524). Smerdyakov then explains the entire sequence of events on the night of Fyodor's murder, explaining how he gained access to Fyodor's house, killed the man, and stole the 3,000 rubles that had been set aside to lure Grushenka to the house. He even shows Ivan the money as evidence. Yet he insists that the entire responsibility for the murder lies on Ivan's shoulders: "you are still responsible for it all, since you knew of the murder, sir, and charged me to do it, sir, and went away knowing all about it. And so I want to prove to your face this evening that you are the only real murderer in the whole affair, sir, and I am not the real murderer, though I did kill him. You are the rightful murderer" (527). Ivan is shaken by this accusation, but he tells Smerdyakov that he will make a full confession at Dmitry's trial and bring Smerdyakov to testify as well.

Smerdyakov's claim that Ivan was the sole murderer and that he, Smerdyakov, was only acting upon Ivan's orders has generated much discussion and debate among Dostoevsky scholars. Some accept Smerdyakov's words at face value, and view Smerdyakov merely as Ivan's creation, one who carries out Ivan's hidden desire for his father's death.[34] Others find more complexity here,[35] and the question of the degree to which Ivan desired, approved of, or ordered his father's murder merits close analysis. One must begin with Smerdyakov himself, and his relationship with Ivan. Clearly, Smerdyakov was fascinated with Ivan, and for a time Ivan apparently encouraged Smerdyakov's devotion. Smerdyakov, the illegitimate child, held in contempt by those around him and acutely aware of his status as a lowly servant in a household where his likely half-brothers are wined and dined, was easily drawn to Ivan's notions about a selected elite of "intelligent" people who seem to have a right to deceive the masses and rule over them because of their superior wisdom and insight. When Smerdyakov gets wind of Ivan's affirmation that "There is no virtue if there is no immortality" (65), he may interpret this as a declarative slogan to live by, not as a tentative hypothesis couched in the subjunctive mode. As Gary Saul Morson succinctly observes, for Smerdyakov, "all statements are in the indicative" ("Verbal Pollution," 229). Indeed, Smerdyakov himself hears Ivan plainly declare: "There is no immortality" (120). Yet Smerdyakov does not perceive, as does Zosima, that this question is not settled in Ivan's mind, and that it continues to fret his heart.

A similar complexity emerges in the question of the degree to which Ivan desired his father's death. Although Ivan may indeed have wished for his father's death at certain moments, he had also pledged to defend his father (though this was spoken to Alyosha, and Smerdyakov may have been unaware of it). In truth, Ivan was deeply conflicted in his feelings toward his father. Though he surely despised the old man at times, it is not clear that he was decisively committed to seeing him dead. His horror at the thought that he could have been responsible for his father's death is absolutely genuine. Ivan's inner doubts and internal struggles, however, are entirely lost on Smerdyakov, and so he carries out Fyodor's murder not only because he believes this is acceptable to Ivan, but because it suits his own desires and designs as well. He feels nothing but resentment toward Fyodor (his victim) and Dmitry (upon whom he wants to pin the murder), and he plans to use the stolen money to start a new life in Moscow or abroad. When he subsequently learns that Ivan is distraught about the murder and his possible culpability, he himself is surprised and disappointed. He reproaches Ivan: "You used to say yourself that everything was permitted, so now why are you so upset, too?" (531). We note that when he quotes Ivan's words, he leaves out the "if" clause about immortality that anchored Ivan's original statement.

Disenchanted that this idol turned out to be so weak, Smerdyakov lashes out at Ivan, and tries to cast all the blame on Ivan himself, perhaps to punish Ivan for his weakness. Although Ivan did not actually "order" Smerdyakov to commit murder, and Dostoevsky himself stated that Ivan participated in the murder "only obliquely and remotely" by not stopping Smerdyakov when he sensed what Smerdyakov intended to do (letter of 8 November 1879; *Complete Letters* 5: 164), Smerdyakov throws this accusation in Ivan's face in a spirit of malicious spite. Now Ivan wants to bring Smerdyakov to justice along with himself, but Smerdyakov will not give him that satisfaction. Instead, he commits suicide without acknowledging his guilt in the murder. This suicide, which may have been motivated in part by his despair at the failure of Ivan to live up to Smerdyakov's ideas and by his own recognition that the murder has not brought the real change in his life he was seeking, is also fueled by spite in that Smerdyakov refuses to provide Ivan and Dmitry with any chance at public absolution.[36]

On the way to his third meeting with Smerdyakov, Ivan had run into a drunken peasant and knocked him into the snow. Thinking that the man would freeze, Ivan made no attempt to help and continued on his way. After he has met with Smerdyakov and resolved to confess his involvement in the crime, he again stumbles upon the peasant, and this time he lifts him up and takes him to a nearby house for help. This image of apparent or near death followed by resurrection or restoration to life recalls the analogous moments in the revelatory experiences that Alyosha and Dmitry underwent earlier in the novel (with Zosima and Grigory in the role of one whose "death" is followed by a kind of resurrection). Yet this peasant is not a cherished surrogate father for Ivan; he is a total stranger. And the agent of both the seeming death and the apparent resurrection is Ivan himself, not God. The "miracle," then, is simply man-made. Nor is there any comforting contact with a compassionate woman, as there had been in Alyosha's and Dmitry's case. What's more, although Ivan's gesture of providing help to one whom he had injured suggests a positive change of heart, he does not follow this up by going immediately to the authorities to confess his knowledge of the murder of his father. Thus, the ensuing revelation that Ivan experiences is not joyous and uplifting, like his brothers'. Rather it is just the opposite: Ivan comes face to face with the devil.

Ivan's meeting with the devil is one of the most distinctive scenes in the novel, and Dostoevsky's two-part chapter title ("The Devil. Ivan Fyodorovich's Nightmare") hints at some ambiguity over the devil's ontological status in the work: is he an authentic denizen of the supernatural world, or is he merely an hallucination produced by Ivan's feverish mind on the heels of his shattering encounter with a real person who has brought Ivan into contact with Ivan's own darkest impulses? This meeting fulfills several functions. Most importantly, perhaps, it forces Ivan to confront the shabbiness and unseemliness of his own ideas. This Dostoevsky accomplishes in two ways: through the physical appearance of the devil and through the devil's mocking restatement of Ivan's ideas themselves.

To begin with, Dostoevsky provides a detailed description of the devil's shabby appearance. Most striking is his characterization as a "toady, a sponger of the best class" who is like one of those "solitary creatures, either bachelors or widowers," who, if they have children, generally leave them in the care of some relative and "gradually lose sight of their children altogether" (534). Such a characterization reminds one of Fyodor Karamazov's own appearance and conduct, and it is highly ironic (and humiliating) that Ivan's devil takes the form of the figure who had aroused in Ivan such loathing and embarrassment. The devil himself acknowledges that his appearance is one of the reasons why Ivan is so displeased with him: "You are really angry with me for not having appeared to you in a red glow, 'with thunder and lightning,' with scorched wings, but have shown myself in such a modest form. You are wounded [...] in your pride. How could such a vulgar devil visit such a great man as you!" (544). As Robert Belknap has shown, Dostoevsky's invention of a shabby devil represents a marvelously original way to debunk the Romantic image of the devil that had been so popular earlier in the century (see his *Genesis*, 132–7).

The devil's satiric treatment of some of Ivan's cherished ideas further humiliates and angers Ivan. Over the course of the encounter, the devil offers up a vision of the universe in which the figure of God seems absent, a sharp refraction of Ivan's vision of an insensitive or absent God in Book Five. The most cutting example of the devil's mockery, however, is the one with which the meeting concludes. The devil offers a summary of Ivan's notions about a time when people will discard their traditional belief in God and ascend to the position of "man-gods" themselves. But if that time does not come, or takes too long to arrive, then perhaps anyone who "recognizes the truth even now may legitimately order his life as he pleases, on the new principles. In that sense, 'all things are permitted' for him" (546). Having touched upon one of the most consequential and fateful phrases in the novel, the devil now reveals that there may be something crude and self-serving behind this philosophy: "That's all very charming; but if you want to swindle why do you want a moral sanction for doing it? But that's our modern Russian all over. He can't bring himself to swindle without a moral sanction" (546). Stung by this cynical debunking of an idea he had once espoused with such pride, Ivan emulates Luther and his inkwell and throws a glass of tea at the devil, thereby ending the encounter.

A second function that the devil's visit to Ivan fulfills has to do with the very question of whether the devil is a real entity or merely a mental projection. Ivan is torn between believing that the devil is his own creation, paltry as it is, and the possibility that the devil, and therefore the entire realm of the supernatural, actually exists. This split, of course, reflects Ivan's desperate uncertainty about whether God and immortality themselves exist. In an interesting twist, the devil claims that he himself would like to join those who light candles in honor of God, and that he is trying to instill a tiny seed of faith in Ivan. To do so, he says, he is applying a "special method" (537), which involves leading Ivan to belief and disbelief by turns. Knowing Ivan's spirit of contradiction, he understands that if he can momentarily goad Ivan into *not* believing, Ivan will immediately begin to assert the contrary and claim that the devil is "not a dream but a reality." As a result, he will sow in Ivan "only a tiny little seed of faith, and out of it will grow an oak tree" (542), a fresh iteration of the agricultural motif introduced in the novel's epigraph. The devil concludes: "One must do a good deed sometimes" (543).

If one considers the devil to be Ivan's creation, the devil's salutary endeavor clearly signals a desire on Ivan's part to find faith and to climb out of the abyss of nihilistic despair in which he has become trapped. Indeed, when Alyosha arrives with news of Smerdyakov's death, Ivan offers disjointed comments about the devil but asserts: "I should be awfully glad to think that it was *he* and not I" (549). This is not merely an attempt to separate himself from the unseemliness of the devil's appearance and gossipy chatter, but an expression of Ivan's desire that the devil, and the entire unearthly dimension that the devil's being might imply, has an authentic existence outside his own mind. As a further sign that Ivan's soul is striving to free itself from the vicious snares of cynicism and doubt, Ivan retracts his mean comments about Liza: "I said something nasty about her. It was a lie. I like her" (549).

Nevertheless, Ivan's soul is still in turmoil, and as he discusses his motivations for going to give testimony against himself at Dmitry's trial (even though Smerdyakov is dead and cannot corroborate his story), he indicates that he is driven to do so out of pride and the fear that he would consider himself cowardly if he did not do so. Although his determination to make a confession suggests a willingness to break out of his self-imposed isolation and assume responsibility for his words and deeds before others, he does not yet evince clear signs of true repentance or remorse. Rather, he feels himself being overcome with spite toward Dmitry and even Alyosha, and he cries out: "Oh, tomorrow I'll go, stand before them, and spit in their faces!" (551). Alyosha recognizes the struggle raging within Ivan, but he retains hope that the struggle will end positively: "'God will conquer!' he thought. 'Either he will rise up in the light of truth, or...he'll perish in hate, revenging on himself and on everyone his having served the cause he does not believe in'" (551).

The trial and the epilogue

Book Twelve focuses on Dmitry's trial and consists mainly of testimony from witnesses (including Ivan's frenzied self-accusation that refers to the devil as his only corroborating witness) and long speeches from the prosecuting and defense attorneys. The narrator's account interweaves moment of high tension with elements of farcical absurdity. Although the defense attorney is more accurate than the prosecutor in his reconstruction of character psychology and possible crime scenarios, even he goes too far in his efforts to win mercy for Dmitry. Arguing that Fyodor was too abusive to earn the designation of "father," the attorney declares that even if Dmitry had killed him in a fit of madness, "[s]uch a murder is not a murder. Such a murder is not a parricide" (624).[37] Despite the attorney's eloquence and acumen, Dmitry is found guilty nonetheless, even though he had not killed his father, and this outcome provides the capstone for the novel's extensive deliberations on justice. As it turns out, human "justice" can be sorely flawed, and Dostoevsky calls into question the assurance with which earthly ["Euclidean"] minds render judgment on others.[38] Clearly, the legal system in its current configuration cannot adequately deal with issues of crime, culpability, and reformation in their full emotional and spiritual dimensions.[39]

Now Dmitry must confront the issue of whether to follow Ivan's plan and escape the punishment that awaits him. He is worried that he will not have the strength to bear the coarseness and violence he imagines lying before him in Siberia. Alyosha tries to console him by saying that the "martyr's cross" is not for Dmitry at this time: "you are innocent, and such a cross is too much for you" (636). As for Dmitry's conviction that he has the potential to become a "new man," Alyosha tells him that the memory of that new man will serve as a guide and goal for his future conduct. Some critics see Alyosha as fulfilling the role of a tempter here. In those readings, Dmitry must go to Siberia and suffer to realize the Christological model that Dostoevsky has shaped for him.[40] Others, however, accept Alyosha's counsel as judicious.[41] Perhaps Dmitry would not need to go to Siberia to become the new man he would like to be.[42] Indeed, as Curt Whitcomb has pointed out, there may be a hazard in pursuing an heroic exploit ("podvig") rather than taking up a more modest and patient penitential path ("Temptation of Miracle," 196–8). Contemplating the latter path, Dmitry envisions going to America and working there with Grushenka for many years, until he can return to Russia with a new identity. America, as Dostoevsky has depicted it in other works, is no paradise. Svidrigailov in *Crime and Punishment* speaks of going to America, and then commits suicide. Shatov and Kirillov in *The Devils* go to America, suffer sorely, and return to Russia. Perhaps for Dmitry, America would serve as a kind of cleansing Purgatory, and his affirmation—"I love Russia, Alyosha, I love the Russian God" (637)—indicates that his heart is firmly in the right place.

At this point, the world of adults in *The Brothers Karamazov* is still seriously unsettled. Dmitry has been sentenced to hard labor in Siberia, but he may attempt an escape. Ivan, according to Alyosha, "is lying at death's door" (644); the prospects for his recovery are uncertain. Thus Dostoevsky turns to the younger generation, and he concludes his novel with a moving depiction of Ilyusha's funeral and Alyosha's speech to the boys by Ilyusha's favorite stone. The funeral scene combines notes of soft grace and evocations of profound grief. The narrator writes of Ilyusha's body: "strange to say there was practically no smell from the corpse" (640). Perhaps miracles appear where least expected. The long-suffering Ilyusha shows no sign of corruption. Lisa Khokhlakova has sent flowers; perhaps her destructive anguish has eased. Captain Snegiryov, however, is understandably heartbroken. When he catches sight of Ilyusha's little boots by the bed, he cries out with grief: "where are your little feet?" (644), and the reader may recall that the peasant woman mourning the death of her child in Book Two also spoke movingly of her boy's "little boots" and "little feet" (47, 48). In the overall design of the novel, these two images of parents grieving over the loss of their children enfold and provide a vivid contrast to Ivan's bitter, dry-eyed tirade about children's suffering. Significantly, Alyosha's response to the sight of Snegiryov's grief echoes Zosima's, and he tells Kolya: "Let them weep" (644).

For the final scene, Dostoevsky turns away from this grief and depicts Alyosha suddenly being inspired to make a speech. For much of the novel he has been the least voluble of the Karamazov brothers, but now he has found his own voice. The thrust of his speech is an invocation to Ilyusha's friends to remember their companion, and he states that one such memory may save

them from great evil. Alyosha's injunction reminds the reader
of Alyosha's own precious memory of his mother, and it echoes
Zosima's teachings on how a seed planted in childhood may
come into bloom at a later date. Alyosha's words excite the boys,
and Kolya, the former would-be Socialist, asks: "can it really be
true what religion says, that we shall all rise from the dead, and
shall live, and see each other again, everyone, and Ilyushechka?"
(646). "Certainly we shall all rise again," responds Alyosha, and
the novel ends with the boys giving Alyosha a rousing cheer. As
Robert Louis Jackson has pointed out, this scene can be read as
Dostoevsky's final response to Ivan's caustic questions about justice
in the universe: "The suffering of the child is ultimately a basis for
union and harmony, both in an immediate and in a higher sense"
("Alyosha's Speech," 237).

The scene of Alyosha's speech has clear religious overtones.
There are about a dozen boys gathered around Alyosha (640), and
his words invoking the children to retain their memory of Ilyusha
resonate with Christ's injunction to his disciples when breaking
bread at the Last Supper: "do this in remembrance of me" (1 Cor.
11.24). The stone at which the speech is given recalls Christ's declaration to Peter that he would be the rock on which Christ would
build his church (Mt. 16.18). (It also caps the "stone" theme in
the novel. From the stones with which Ilyusha and the other boys
hurled at each other, we have moved to the stone at which their
friendship is eternally solidified.) Of course, although Dostoevsky
intends to associate Alyosha with the model established by Christ,
he does not seek to make the identification absolute. For one thing,
Alyosha is not calling upon the children to do anything in memory
of *him*; rather, they are to remember *Ilyusha*, and, in the eyes of
some readers, it is the dead boy who is the "symbolic equivalent
of the dead Christ" in whose memory a new community will be
formed (see Rimvydas Silbajoris, "Children," 37). The religious
notes in this episode are meant to lift the reader out of the squalid
world of the Karamazov family and toward a new realm with a
promising future. The biological Karamazov family has dissolved;
a new family, united along different lines, is coming into being.
For the moment at least, one can let go of strife and turmoil and
envision something better to come. Dostoevsky concludes his tale
with a shimmering evocation of that new beginning.

Study questions

1   The murder of a father is a central plot element in *The Brothers Karamazov*. This points to the importance of the theme of fatherhood in the novel. What about motherhood? What role do mothers play? How is their presence or absence felt in the novel?

2   Ivan's tale of the Grand Inquisitor is sometimes published as an individual work separate from the novel in which it appears. What are the consequences of this type of separate publication? What might readers of the tale be missing if they read it in isolation?

3   Some readers regard Smerdyakov as a demonic entity. Is he truly demonic, or does his character result from abuse and neglect? How should the reader understand Smerdyakov's status in the text?

4   Do you think that Ivan wanted someone to murder his father? Did he order Smerdyakov to do so? What is his relationship to Smerdyakov?

5   Dostoevsky hoped that his novel as a whole would provide an effective response to Ivan's challenge to the divine order of the cosmos. Do you think the novel responds effectively to Ivan's challenge or not?

Notes

1   Indeed, it is worth noting that Dostoevsky himself had put forth an idea bearing a strong similarity to Ivan's theory. In his December 1876 entry of *A Writer's Diary*, Dostoevsky wrote: "I declare [...] that love for humanity is even entirely unthinkable, incomprehensible, and *utterly impossible without faith in the immortality of the human soul to go along with it*" (*A Writer's Diary* 1: 736; emphasis in the original).

2   The word *smerd* in Russian also meant a low-born individual or a serf. That this word is also present in Smerdyakov's name underscores his status as a lackey (and his treatment as such) in the Karamazov household.

3   For an interesting discussion of the importance of Smerdyakov's "neglected brotherhood" and the way that Dostoevsky implicates the reader in his characters' neglect of Smerdyakov see Olga Meerson's chapter entitled "The Fourth Brother" in her book *Dostoevsky's Taboos*. See also Anna Berman, "Siblings," 277–81.

4   For a discussion of models of confession in the novel, see Julian Connolly, "Confession in *The Brothers Karamazov*."

5   For a discussion of the significance of Schiller in Dostoevsky's work, see Alexandra Lyngstad, *Dostoevskij and Schiller*.

6   Ksana Blank discusses the Demester–Persephone saga in relation to Dmitry's experiences in *Dostoevsky's Dialectics and the Problem of Sin*, 41–51.

7   Robert Louis Jackson provides an important clarification on Dmitry's assertion: "to Dostoevsky it is not beauty that is ambivalent, but man who experiences two kinds of beauty—not only the true, higher beauty, but also a low order of aesthetic sensation [...] which *he* calls beauty [...] The aesthetic confusion is in *man*" (*Dostoevsky's Quest for Form*, 64; emphasis in original).

8   Alyosha's question is usually translated as "Will *my* brother Dmitry soon be back" (emphasis added), but the Russian original omits the personal pronoun, thereby opening up some ambiguity about the referent in Alyosha's question: the unmodified word "brother" may trigger Smerdyakov's own sensitivity to the issue of his unacknowledged status as half-brother to both Dmitry and Alyosha.

9   An entry in the *Povest' vremennykh let* (known in English as the *Russian Primary Chronicle*) under the year 6494 (986) reads: "Satan entered into Cain and incited Cain to kill Abel." See *The Nikonian Chronicle From the Beginning to the Year 1132 (Volume One)*, (ed.) Serge A. Zenkovsky (Princeton: The Kingston Press, 1984), 83.

10 Diane Thompson adds that in this conversation at the tavern, Ivan "took the devil's side" (*Poetics of Memory*, 149). For a detailed discussion of Ivan's association with the demonic, see Julian Connolly, "Conflict at the Crisis Point: *The Brothers Karamazov*," 204–31.

11 See, for example, Kenneth Surin's discussion of Ivan's arguments in "The Critique of Traditional Theodicy: The Case of Ivan Karamazov," and Dan R. Stiver's discussion in "Still Too High a Price? Ivan's Question in the Light of Contemporary Theodicy."

12 For an illuminating discussion of how closely Dostoevsky's own views on the horrors of child abuse were aligned with Ivan's, see Susan McReynolds, *Redemption and the Merchant God*, 157–98.

13   Liza Knapp offers an insightful discussion of Dostoevsky's
      appreciation of the possibilities opened up by the admission of
      non-Euclidean space in her book *Annihilation of Inertia*, 185–98.
      Ralph C. Wood argues that because of his Western orientation,
      Ivan fails to appreciate the Orthodox conception of the creation "as
      the very icon of God" and therefore does not realize that human
      suffering "in the visible world cannot be understood apart from the
      redemption being wrought in the invisible world"("Dostoevsky on
      Evil as a Perversion of Personhood" [4, 8]).

14   Ellis Sandoz finds it ironic that the Grand Inquisitor chastises others
      for their weakness when he himself is "too weak" for authentic faith
      (*Political Apocalypse*, 155).

15   Roger Cox has argued that it is actually the Grand Inquisitor
      who rejects miracle, mystery, and authority, and proposes instead
      "magic, mystification, and tyranny" (*Between Earth and Heaven*,
      195).

16   Dostoevsky himself wrote about a particular twist in human
      psychology in which one who has to witness the suffering of a
      loved one can over time begin to hate that person, and he stated:
      "I maintain that the awareness of one's own inability to assist or
      bring any aid or relief at all to suffering humanity, coupled with
      one's complete conviction of the exitence of that suffering, can
      even *transform the love for humanity in your heart to hatred for
      humanity*" (*Writer's Diary* 1: 735). Perhaps Ivan's Grand Inquisitor
      has succumbed to this phenomenon, unable to find the inner
      strength to continue to love humanity in the face of the suffering he
      sees in it.

17   In Russian folk belief, the devil stands on a person's left side and
      whispers evil suggestions in the person's left ear. See Maksimov,
      Nechistaia, nevedomaia i krestnaia sila, 14.

18   A detailed account of Zosima's relationship to religious and literary
      antecedents is found in Sven Linnér's *Starets Zosima in The Brothers
      Karamazov: A Study in the Mimesis of Virtue*.

19   Gary L. Browning traces the numerous variations of this formula
      in the novel and argues that the word translated as "responsible"
      ("vinovat") should properly be translated as "guilty," foregrounding
      the religious and mystical connotations of the word ("Zosima's
      'Secret,'" 527n. 2).

20   Robert Belknap asserted that the Book of Job was the "greatest"
      theodicy Dostoevsky knew (*Genesis*, 137). Yet Harold Bloom
      declared that Zosima's interpretation of the Book of Job is "the

weakest failure in the history of theodicy," and he declares that it is
difficult to answer the Grand Inquisitor "with such sublime idiocy"
("Introduction" to *Fyodor Dostoevsky's* The Brothers Karamazov,
4). Susan McReynolds argues that there really is no "mystery" at
all here. Zosima's interpretation of Job's story relies on "exchange
logic": in place of his dead children Job receives new ones and
comes to love them. McReynolds points out that Zosima's exegesis
does not address the meaning of "innocent suffering"; rather he
deals with "the issue of the survivors' response to it" (*Redemption*,
164, 165).

21   For a fascinating analysis of the palpable costs and intangible
     benefits brought out in this confessional episode, see Caryl
     Emerson's essay "Zosima's 'Mysterious Visitor.'"

22   Yet as the second half of the tale warns, the choice to do good or
     evil will recur. One must constantly strive to make the right choice.
     Grushenka's inclusion of the entire story may signal her own
     uncertainty about how she will conduct herself in the future. For a
     discussion of this episode, see Smyth, "The 'Lukovka' Legend'"; and
     Morson, "The God of Onions."

23   Quoted in Steven Cassedy, *Dostoevsky's Religion*, 116.

24   Ibid., 118.

25   Sergei Hackel has observed that Dostoevsky refers to the
     Transfiguration in his notebooks (see *Notebooks*, 95), although not
     explicitly in this novel. ("The Religious Dimension," 152)

26   These figures suggest to Veselin Kesich a religious icon of Mary and
     Jesus ("Some Religious Aspects," 98n. 6), and the scene will remind
     some readers of Alyosha's memory of his mother stretching toward a
     similar icon.

27   Carol Flath also finds parallels between the overt miracle that
     takes place in the Gospel account of the Cana of Galilee episode
     and the implicit miracle tht occurs at Mokroe ("*Passion* of Dmitrii
     Karamazov," 596–7). See also Roger B. Anderson, "The Meaning
     of Carnival in *The Brothers Karamazov*," 467–73. For further
     analysis of the epiphanic scenes in the novel, see Julian Connolly,
     "Dostoevsky's Guide to Spiritual Epiphany in *The Brothers
     Karamazov*."

28   The phrase "centered on action" was used by A. Boyce Gibson
     (*The Religion of Dostoevsky*, 186), and Steven Cassedy noted that
     for Dostoevsky a Christian ministry "takes place in this world"
     (*Dostoevsky's Religion*, 155). Unlike Dmitry at the outset of the
     novel, Alyosha is already oriented toward helping others, and

Zosima's injunction to him to leave the monaster and "serve" (71) only reinforces this orientation.

29 Robert Belknap states that Kolya's behavior "trivializes" the ideas of the Grand Inquisitor, and that in doing so, he "cheapens" Ivan and his lofty fantasies (*Genesis*, 149, 150).

30 For a discussion of this episode in the broader context of the novel as a whole, see Maxim Shrayer's essay, "The Jewish Question and *The Brothers Karamazov*."

31 Susanne Fusso speculates that Ivan has become the main object of Liza's "depraved mental life" and her sexual frustration (*Discovering Sexuality in Dostoevsky*, 78). See also Diane Oenning Thompson's discussion in "Lise Khokhlakova: *shalunia / besenok*."

32 The Russian word Liza uses to characterize herself is "podlaia," and her usage of this word recalls the word Ivan used to abuse himself after deciding to flee to Moscow rather than stay home and defend his father—"podlets."

33 For further discussion of this scene and Aloysha's role as would be confessor and healer, see Julian Connolly, "Confession in *The Brothers Karamazov*."

34 See, for example, Edward Wasiolek's discussion of the relationship in *Dostoevsky: The Major Fiction* (172–5).

35 See, for example, Vladimir Kantor's analysis in his essay "Pavel Smerdyakov and Ivan Karamazov: The Problem of Tempation."

36 Michael Holquist writes that Smerdyakov committed suicide "not out of fear of capture, but from the despair of a twice-abandoned orphan" (*Dostoevsky and the Novel*, 182). Then too, Smerdyakov had never shown a Karamazovian love of life. Earlier in the novel he declared: "I would have sanctioned their killing me before I was born that I might not have come into the world at all" (194).

37 In the February 1876 installment of his *Writer's Diary*, Dostoevsky himself had written about the trial of a father who was accused (and acquitted) of child abuse, and he argued there that the family is "*created*, not provided ready-made"; it is created "by a ceaseless labor of love" (*Writer's Diary* 1: 381). He would not, however, go so far as to justify parricide.

38 Richard Peace even declares that the "human conception of justice is […] a travesty of the word" (*Dostoevsky*, 281).

39 For a detailed discussion of Dmitry's trial in light of Dostoevsky's views on the legal system, see Rosenshield, *Western Law, Russian Justice*, 131–253.

40 See, for example, Flath ("The *Passion* of Dmitrii Karamazov," 595–6) and Rosenshield (*Western Law, Russian Justice*, 211–12, 226–31).

41 See, for example, Thompson, *Poetics of Memory*, 279.

42 Paul Contino lays out just such an argument in his essay on the escape plan, "Incarnational Realism and the Case for Casuistry: Dmitry Karamazov's Escape."

CHAPTER FOUR

Critical reception, composition, and publishing history

Dostoevsky's work on the novel

Although Dostoevsky had been exploring some of the major themes to be treated in *The Brothers Karamazov* for many years (in his *Diary of a Writer* and elsewhere), he began working in earnest on this specific project in the spring and summer of 1878. The notes he made at the time indicate that his conceptions about the main characters had not yet found their final form. For example, the prototype for the character that would ultimately become Alyosha Karamazov is referred to in some notes as the "Idiot" (see *Notebooks*, 4). While writing the novel, Dostoevsky was affected by events in the world around him and in his personal life, such as the death of his young son Alyosha (Alexey) in May 1878, and his subsequent visit to the Optyna Pustyn' monastery with the philosopher Vladimir Solovyov. He incorporated elements of these experiences into his novel.

By July 1878, he could declare to a correspondent: "I have now begun my novel and am working on it, but it's far from finished.

It's only just been started" (11 July 1978; *Complete Letters* 5: 51). At that time, he envisioned writing a novel that would appear in serial form over the course of a year. Yet although he turned in the first two books of his novel to the editors of the *Russian Messenger* (*Russkii vestnik*) in November 1878 and they appeared in the January 1879 issue of the journal, it would be nearly two years before the final installment of the novel was published.

While he worked on the novel, Dostoevsky would write his editor N. A. Lyubimov to let him know how the project was coming along. These letters, which were intended to shape Lyubimov's response to the evolving scope and content of the novel as it was being written and submitted, offer intriguing insight into what Dostoevsky himself regarded as significant and worthy of comment. It is noteworthy, for example, that Dostoevsky conceptualized each book somewhat as a self-contained whole. He wrote to Lyubimov that everything "will be in finished form for each book. That is, no matter how small or large the fragment, it will contain something whole and finished" (30 April 1879; *Complete Letters* 5: 79). Through these letters, Dostoevsky not only explained his essential conception, he made special requests to preserve specific word choices, even if they sounded a bit rude and could make the censors uncomfortable (for example, he begged Lyubimov to keep the phrase "the cherubim's hysterical shrieks" in the devil's discourse with Ivan, but he would tolerate "joyful shouts" if absolutely necessary [10 August 1880; *Complete Letters* 5: 262]).

As Dostoevsky continued his efforts on the novel, he realized that his original plan of publishing the novel in one year's time would not be feasible, and he warned Lyubimov of this in a letter written 8 July 1879. Not only did he cite health problems, but he indicated that his overall conception of the scope and breadth of the novel had grown. In a subsequent letter (written on 16 November 1879), he described how he decided to add a section dealing with Dmitry's arrest and preliminary interrogation, and felt the need to provide more detail and context for what would culminate in Dmitry's regenerative dream. The writer was chagrined that he would disappoint those readers expecting the novel to be finished by year's end, so he penned a special letter to the editor for publication in the journal, in which he apologized to his readers, taking full blame on himself, and absolving the journal of the suspicion that the delay in publishing the novel was some kind of commercial ploy.

Dostoevsky's sensitivity to his readers' potential reactions also showed up in letters he wrote to readers who had questions about the novel as it was appearing. To one reader who was mystified as to what happened after Dmitry pulled the brass pestle out of his pocket as he observed his father with growing revulsion in Book Eight, Dostoevsky offered a detailed summary and analysis: "The old man Karamazov was killed by the servant Smerdyakov [...] Ivan Fyodorovich participated in the murder only obliquely and remotely, only by (intentionally) keeping from bringing Smerdyakov to his senses during the conversation with him before his departure for Moscow [...] and thus *seemed to permit* Smerdyakov to commit the crime [...] Dmitry Fydorovich is completely innocent of the murder" (8 November 1879; *Complete Letters* 5: 164).[1]

With additional delays and complications, it was not until 8 November 1880 that Dostoevsky could send off the final installment of the novel and declare to Lyubimov: "Well, and so the novel is finished! I have worked on it for three years, spent two publishing it—this is a significant moment for me" (*Complete Letters* 5: 290–1). Interestingly, when Dostoevsky published the novel as a self-standing edition (in two volumes) in December 1880, he made few changes to the text, even allowing to stand a typographer's error in which part of the Grand Inquisitor's monologue was not broken up into separate paragraphs as Dostoevsky had originally intended.

Early reviews

Because *The Brothers Karamazov* appeared serially over nearly two years' time, critical reviews and notes on the novel began appearing long before the entire novel had seen daylight. In 1879 alone, over thirty such reviews appeared in the periodical press. Calling these reviews "[t]erse," "tentative," and "often tendentious," William Mills Todd III explicates the function of the reviews that came out while the novel was still in the early stages of publication: "these newspaper reviews would begin to mediate between writer and public immediately, helping to shape contemporary opinion and providing 'feed-back' for the writer while he was still planning and composing the novel" ("Contexts of Criticism," 295, 294).

Contemporary responses to the novel often reflected the ideological stance of the critic and journal in which the review appeared. Some in the liberal press criticized Dostoevsky for promoting what the reviewers saw as mysticism. One critic, writing in the journal *Russian Truth* (*Russkaia Pravda*) in June 1879, lamented that "[t]hose pages of the novel on which the 'elders' of the monastery appear before the reader surrounded by a shining aura of unearthly grandeur and unearthly wisdom can hardly arouse anything other than pity for a writer whose near-genius talent cannot break free from the snares of mysticism" (cited in *PSS* 15: 489). Others chided Dostoevsky for exposing the seamy side of life: "Having depicted too assiduously the stinking filth of depravity, the author shows us in virtue only the absence of this filth [...] Where is health? In vain do we seek it in the novel [...] We see only pathological phenomena."[2]

Even some who were more sympathetic to the religious content of the novel had their reservations about certain aspects of Dostoevsky's creation. Konstantin Leontiev, for example, asserted in his essay "On Universal Love" in 1880 that although Dostoevsky had drawn closer to the Orthodox "Church" in his latest novel (as compared with his earlier work), the novel still did not portray the religious life of the Orthodox monastery in sufficient detail. While truly mystical feelings were expressed weakly, feelings of "humanitarian idealization," even in the speeches of the monks, were expressed "very ardently and at length" ("O vsemirnoi liubvi," 198). Nonetheless, the novel appeared more satisfactory to Leontiev than Dostoevsky's 1880 Pushkin speech, which seemed too "European" in its ideas and origin ("O vsemirnoi liubvi," 200).

Despite these notes of criticism, many contemporary readers acknowledged the literary power and vibrancy of the work. Reacting to the depiction of Zosima in Book Six, V. F. Korsh wrote that Zosima's "Life" "glitters with talent on every page."[3] Even a critic who did not like the monastery episodes of the novel had to acknowledge that in his earlier work, Dostoevsky had never attained "such stunning lyricism, such profound psychological truth and, finally, such artistic truth" as he had in this novel.[4]

Pro et contra

The debate among Russian writers and critics about the meaning of Dostoevsky's artistic legacy, and of *The Brothers Karamazov* in particular, became more substantive in the years after his death. In 1882, the Populist critic Nikolay K. Mikhailovsky published an extended essay under a title that would later be frequently cited in reference to Dostoevsky: "A Cruel Talent." Dismissing those who might unreservedly valorize Dostoevsky's work, Mikhailovsky focused on what he saw as Dostoevsky's core characteristic as a writer: cruelty. "To begin with, it must be noted that cruelty and torture always preoccupied Dostoevsky, and they did so precisely for their attractiveness, for the sensuality which torture seems to contain" (*Cruel Talent*, 11). "[I]t is precisely in the sphere of torture and torment that Dostoevsky's talent achieved its greatest power" (*Cruel Talent*, 50). In Mikhailovsky's view, the "humanistic" element that had featured prominently in Dostoevsky's early work diminished over time, until finally, *The Brothers Karamazov*, along with *The Devils*, became "replete with gratuitous cruelty" (*Cruel Talent*, 47). In *The Brothers Karamazov*, Alyosha stood out as the "most normal person" in a "collection of monsters" (*Cruel Talent*, 65).

Although Mikhailovsky's perspective was particularly grim, he was not alone in pointing to a dark side in Dostoevsky's talent. The writer Vasily Rozanov devoted an entire essay to Ivan Karamazov and his "Legend" about the Grand Inquisitor ("The Legend of the Grand Inquisitor," 1891). Rozanov calls the "Legend" "the most poisonous drop ever to fall to earth" (*Dostoevsky and the Legend*, 208). Acknowledging Dostoevsky to be "the most profound analyst of the human soul" (*Dostoevsky and the Legend*, 51), Rozanov offers a penetrating dissection of Ivan's spiritual malaise and his rejection of God's universe, and he finds in it a profound expression of Dostoevsky's own troubled quest to maintain his faith in the face of human suffering that calls into doubt the very meaning of human life.

At the turn of the century (1901–2), the writer and critic Dmitry Merezhkovsky devoted a series of essays to an analysis of the artistic and religious differences between Leo Tolstoy and Fyodor Dostoevsky, and coining a memorable phrase, he called Tolstoy the "seer of the flesh" ("tainovidets ploti") and Dostoevsky the "seer of the spirit" ("tainovidets dukha").[5] Reacting to earlier critics of Dostoevsky's work, he chided those who saw in Dostoevsky only a "cruel talent," and he declared that the writer's apparent cruelty simply masked his quest for knowledge (*Tvorchestvo*, 105, 108). Characterizing Dostoevsky's works not as novels or epics, but as tragedies, Merezhkovsky hailed many features of the work, including Alyosha's epiphanic vision in *The Brothers Karamazov*, which Merezhkovsky deemed an authentic act of seeing, as Dostoevsky created feelings within Alyosha like those within the disciples who viewed the resurrected Christ. Merezhkovsky declared Dostoevsky to be the herald of a new religion and a true prophet, thereby setting the tone for several later Russian critics (*Tvorchestvo*, 165).

Thus, Sergey N. Bulgakov published in 1902 an essay entitled "Ivan Karamazov as a Philosophical Type" (presented as a speech the year before). Bulgakov delineated affinities between Ivan's concept of the "god-man" and Friedrich Nietzsche's "Übermensch" [literally, "overman"], and he saw both men struggling with the implications of "atheistic amoralism" ("Ivan Karamazov," 24). Yet while Nietzsche went mad, and Ivan also suffered a psychic illness, Dostoevsky himself rose above this, as evidenced in the creation of Alyosha and Zosima. Bulgakov also compared Ivan to Goethe's Faust as one who expresses the torments and doubts of his day. Viewing Ivan as a child of socialism evincing aspects of universality, Bulgakov also saw in Ivan's concern with the suffering around him a truly Russian trait, and he concluded his essay with the remark that such a concern continued to be relevant in the Russia of the current epoch. In the next year Lev Shestov published a book entitled *Dostoevsky and Nietzsche: The Philosophy of Tragedy*. Shestov, who endorsed Mikhailovsky's characterization of Dostoevsky as a "cruel talent," offered an idiosyncratic attempt to link Dostoevsky and Nietzsche as philosophers of tragedy whose aim was not to teach humility, submission, or renunciation, but rather to point out and to champion the ugliness of unvarnished reality.

In a particularly rich reading of Dostoevsky's major fiction published in 1911 ("Dostoevsky and the Novel–Tragedy"), the poet and philosopher Vyacheslav Ivanov explored the artistic representations with which Dostoevsky expressed his deeply

Orthodox Christian worldview. Arguing that the basic conception of Dostoevsky's novels was "thoroughly and essentially tragic," he identified a recurring structural pattern in which "[f]ear and tormenting pity" lead to "an uplifting and liberating final convulsion of the spirit" (*Freedom and the Tragic Life*, 9, 13). In Ivanov's symbolic reading, the portraits of the three Karamazov brothers represent three aspects of Russia herself, and the novel's conclusion depicts a new communal brotherhood bound together by Christ through the child-martyr Ilyusha. The Russian philosopher Nikolay Berdyaev also wrote on Dostoevsky's vision of Christianity, and in his 1923 book entitled *Dostoevsky's Worldview*, he declared that Dostoevsky was "not only a great artist but the greatest of Russia's metaphysicians" (*Dostoevsky*, 218). Berdyaev's particular interest lay in Dostoevsky's treatment of the problem of human freedom. If Dostoevsky can be considered cruel, it is only because he would not "relieve man of his burden of freedom"—the freedom to choose evil as well as good (*Dostoevsky*, 67). Berdyaev found the tale of the Grand Inquisitor to be the "high point" of Dostoevsky's work because it is "a veritable revelation of Christian freedom," "directed much more against godless and materialist socialism" than against Catholicism (*Dostoevsky*, 188, 210, 200).

Addressing Dostoevsky from a very different perspective was the writer Maxim Gorky (Alexey Peshkov). Gorky's occasional commentaries on Dostoevsky, which spanned the period from 1905 to 1934, established a line of approach to Dostoevsky that would eventually come to prevail in the Soviet Union. Viewing Dostoevsky as an artist of contradictions who created compelling portraits of a bourgeois society in distress, Gorky chided Dostoevsky for his ideologically suspect ideas about the road to human reformation. Gorky's early essay "Notes on the Petit Bourgeoisie" (1905) sharply criticized both Dostoevsky and Tolstoy for preaching philosophies of patience (Dostoevsky) and non-violent resistance to evil (Tolstoy) at a time when the Russian people were being sorely oppressed. Gorky returned to this tendentious approach in two short pieces entitled "On Karmazovism" (1913) and "Again on Karamazovism" (1913), in which he criticized the Moscow Art Theater for mounting a stage adaptation of Dostoevsky's novel *The Devils*. Calling Fyodor Karamazov Dostoevsky's "central and most finely understood character," Gorky argued that the representation of Dostoevsky's characters on stage would be harmful to society ("O 'karamazovshchine,'" 67). Two decades later, at a speech delivered to the First All-Union Congress of Soviet Writers (1934), he again damned Dostoevsky with faint praise, calling him an indisputable "genius," but one whose ideas had been inculcated by capitalism and who could easily be imagined in "the role of a medieval inquisitor" ("Soviet Literature," 247).

Before this line was firmly established in the Soviet Union, however, that country witnessed a rise of interest in Dostoevsky's works. In comparison to what was to come, the early and mid-1920s were a time of relative openness in literary criticism. Several distinguished scholars published and commented on newly released materials, prepared editions of Dostoevsky's artistic works, and provided new studies on the writer. These scholars include Leonid Grossman, Arkady Dolinin, and, a little later, Georgy Chulkov. Other scholars, such as Yury Tynyanov and Victor Vinogradov, approached Dostoevsky from a Formalist standpoint and provided detailed studies of Dostoevsky's style and his relationship to his literary predecessors. These studies culminated in Mikhail Bakhtin's seminal monograph *Problems of Dostoevsky's Art* (1929), which was later revised and published with the title *Problems of Dostoevsky's Poetics* (1963). Bakhtin's exploration of the polyphonic nature of Dostoevsky's verbal art showed exquisite sensitivity to the subtle yet dynamic interplay of voices among characters, and among the characters and their narrators.

In the 1930s, however, the ideological battle lines hardened, and with increasing emphasis placed on the production of ideologically correct works of literature and criticism, Dostoevsky's art was regarded with more suspicion than ever. The earlier debate over whether Dostoevsky's humanism and sympathy for the downtrodden outweighed his reactionary antipathy to socialism and the Russian revolutionary movement was decisively settled in favor of those who saw more danger than good in Dostoevsky's work. The abundant flow of Dostoevsky scholarship began to dry up, and relatively few studies of critical distinction appeared in the Soviet Union for two decades (with a brief respite during Second World War).[6] What writing did appear tended to reflect the dominant political tone of the day. One can contrast the entry on Dostoevsky written by A. V. Luncharsky in the first edition of the *Great Soviet Encyclopedia* (1931) with the unsigned entry found in the second edition (1952). Lunacharsky's article highlighted many positive features of Dostoevsky's work, although he too warned that "to pass through this fiery haze, across these dark abysses [...] the reader must be clad in the armor of mature class consciousness."[7] The later entry came to an even harsher conclusion: "Soviet writers and Soviet literary criticism are continuing to fight against the reactionary aspects of Dostoevsky's works and their canonization by the arms-bearers of foreign reaction."[8] Only during the 1956 "Thaw," which happened to coincide with the 125th anniversary of Dostoevsky's birth, were the floodgates of Dostoevsky criticism reopened, and critical interest in Dostoevsky continues to flourish in Russia to the present day.[9]

International fame

In the meantime, Dostoevsky's work had been discovered in the West, and his reputation there was steadily growing. One of the first people to bring attention to Dostoevsky after his death was the French diplomat, the Vicomte E. Melchior de Vogüé, who wrote a study of Russian literature, *Le roman russe*, which came out in 1886 and was soon translated into English. De Vogüé's book championed the Russian novel and served to introduce Dostoevsky to many Western readers for the first time. The Frenchman's point of view on Dostoevsky is clear from the outset. His chapter on Dostoevsky, "The Religion of Suffering," begins with the breathless exclamation: "Here comes the Scythian, the true Scythian, who is going to revolutionize all our intellectual habits!" (*The Russian Novel*, 204). Yet though de Vogüé piqued his readers' interest in Dostoevsky, for many years the English-language reader had to make do with early translations of Dostoevsky's *Notes from the Dead House* (1881) and *Crime and Punishment* (1886), and copies of Dostoevsky's novels in French. In 1909 Maurice Baring published an essay on Dostoevsky that subsequently became a chapter in his book *Landmarks in Russian Literature* (1910). Placing Dostoevsky on a par with Tolstoy (and "immeasurably above" the more well-known Turgenev), Baring finds a "sweet reasonableness" in the author's nature that "pervaded his writings with fragrance like some precious balm"; consequently, Dostoevsky's works "bring comfort to the reader instead of gloom, hope instead of despair" (*Landmarks*, 130, 155, 165). In Baring's opinion, *The Brothers*

Karamazov contains "the whole of Dostotevsky's philosophy and ideas," and it therefore "can be recommended to a hermit who wishes to ponder over something deep, in a cell or on a desert island, to a philosopher who wishes to sharpen his thoughts against a hard whetstone, to a man who is unhappy and wishes to find some healing balm, or to a man who is going on a railway journey and wishes for an exciting story to while away the time" (*Landmarks*, 250).

Although Baring's book whetted the appetitè of English readers, it was only with the publication of Constance Garnett's translation of *The Brothers Karamazov* in 1912 that Dostoevsky became a central topic of conversation among them. The novel triggered many reviews, which often characterized Dostoevsky as revealing to the West the Russian "soul," in all its breadth and strangeness. A veritable Dostoevky cult developed in England. There, J. A. T. Lloyd published in 1912 the first book-length study in English of Dostoevsky, whom he called "the Russian voice of the nineteenth century" (*Great Russian Realist*, 282), and this was followed up by John Middleton Murry's rapturous monograph, *Fyodor Dostoevsky: A Critical Study* (1916). Murry was not particularly interested in Dostoevsky's biography, for, as he wrote:"... fantastic as it may sound, Dostoevsky existed more truly as an idea than as a man. He was a consciousness incarnate [...] From the first he was rather a mind brooding on life than a living man" (*Dostoevsky*, 52). In *The Brothers Karamazov*, Dostoevsky gathered "all the thought, the doubt, and the faith of a lifetime, into one timeless survey of life itself" (*Dostoevsky*, 218). Believing that Dostoevsky's heroes represented consciousnesses and not living lives, Murry offered an unusual interpretation of Ivan Karamazov's relationship to Smerdyakov and the murder of his father: "It may be that Smerdyakov too was a projection of Ivan's own brain." If so, "[i]t may be there really was no Smerdyakov as there really was no Devil, and they both had their abode in Ivan's soul. But then who did the murder? Then of course it may have been Ivan himself, or, on the other hand, there may have been no murder at all" (*Dostoevsky*, 227, 228).

While England experienced a sudden enthusiasm for Russia, and for Dostoevsky in particular (new translations of Dostoevsky's works and biographical materials appeared in significant number), not everyone succumbed to the cult. D. H. Lawrence, who had been a close friend of Murry's, was disappointed with the latter's embrace of the Russian writer.[10] He found in Dostoevsky conflicting impulses toward sensuality and selflessness or spiritual renunciation. In his reading of Dostoevsky, "Christian ecstasy leads to imbecility" and "sensual ecstasy leads to universal murder" (17 February 1916; *Letters*, 331). In Lawrence's opinion, Dostoevsky depicted his characters as "fallen angels," whereas for Lawrence himself, people are "merely people." Thus, Dostoevsky's novels are "great parables" but "false art" (*Letters*, 331). Writing to Murry about Murry's book, Lawrence was even more disdainful: "Dostoevsky, like the rest, can nicely stick his head between the feet of Christ, and waggle his behind in the air. And though the behind-wagglings are a revelation, I don't think much even of the feet of Christ as a bluff for the cowards to hide their eyes against" (28 August 1916; *Letters*, 369). Yet when he was asked to write an introduction to a new translation of the Legend of the Grand Inquisitor, Lawrence agreed to do so. As he saw it, the Grand Inquisitor's view of humanity's essential limitations was accurate, but Lawrence disagreed with Dostoevsky's belief that to evaluate human weakness in this way meant that one was in league with the devil. Lawrence declared that in Dostoevsky, "amazing perspicacity is mixed with ugly perversity." For Lawrence, Dostoevsky "is always perverse, always impure, always an evil thinker and a marvelous seer" ("Introduction," 10).

The debate over Dostoevsky's merits and deficiencies (especially from the formal point of view) continued in England for some time, with writers from Virginia Woolf to Joseph Conrad and Henry James weighing in, either in print or in private letters. Woolf waxed poetic about the Russian soul in Dostoevsky in her essay "The Russian Point of View" (1925): "The novels of Dostoevsky are seething whirlpools, gyrating sandstorms, waterspouts which hiss and boil and suck us in. They are composed purely and wholly of the stuff of the soul [...] He cannot restrain himself. Out it tumbles upon us, hot, scalding, mixed, marvelous, terrible, oppressive—the human soul" (178, 180). Joseph Conrad took a cooler position: in an April 1917 letter to Constance Garnett's husband Edward, he called Dostoevsky a "grimacing terror haunted creature" (*Collected Letters* 6: 78).[11] As time passed, however, more even-handed assessments of Dostoevsky's life and work would make an appearance in the English-speaking world. An example of this is Edward H. Carr's

1931 biography of Dostoevsky, of which D. S. Mirsky, writing in the preface, declared: "There is no nonsense in Mr. Carr's book, and this is probably the first book on the subject (published outside Russia) of which so much can be asserted" ("Preface").

While the English press saw a lively and sustained exchange of views on Dostoevsky, the response on the Continent varied. In 1923, André Gide published a book consisting of lectures he had given on Dostoevsky in 1922, supplemented by earlier writings. Gide ranged widely over Dostoevsky's work, often comparing him with other European writers to highlight the salient features of the Russian's art. Scant attention was paid to *The Brothers Karamazov*, however, as Gide returned repeatedly to *The Devils*. One of the central traits that Gide identified was a remarkable duality of personality in which the two sides of a character's personality find simultaneous expression. Gide anticipated Bakhtin when he wrote that Dostoevsky's theories are articulated in his characters' speeches, rather than in his own voice, and that "[h]is ideas are practically never absolute, remaining relative always to the characters expressing them" (*Dostoevsky*, 92). After Gide, other French intellectuals plumbed Dostoevsky's ideas, most notably the Existentialists. Albert Camus, for example, explored Ivan Karamazov's rebellion in *The Rebel* (1951), focusing on the logical dilemma Ivan found himself in: "Ivan only offers us the tortured face of the rebel plunged in the abyss, incapable of action, torn between the idea of his own innocence and the desire to kill" (*Rebel*, 56).

In Germany, Dostoevsky's work attracted the attention of several prominent figures. Although Friedrich Nietzsche had little sympathy for Dostoevsky's embrace of Christianity, he also wrote in *Twilight of the Idols* (1889) that Dostoevsky was "the only psychologist [...] from whom I had anything to learn" (99). German interest in Dostoevsky reached a peak in the late 1910s and early-1920s. In 1921, his works sold over 200,000 copies (Krinitsyn, "Dostoevskii v Germanii," 181). For many German intellectuals, Dostoevsky's work offered a fascinating glimpse into a world of psychological, emotional, and spiritual intensity that seemed monumental in its scope and suggestiveness. Stefan Zweig, for one, wrote a deeply appreciative commentary on Dostoevsky's work in 1920, in which he tried to convey the "awe," "dread," and "mystery" that Dostoevsky's work inspired (*Three Masters*,

101). The key to understanding Dostoevsky, Zweig stated, was to fathom his emotional "polarity": swinging between the extremes of joy and pain, Dostoevsky the artist became "the greatest dualist, that art, and maybe humanity, has ever known" (*Three Masters*, 133). Within Dostoevsky "was resurrected [...] the bard of a mystic age, the sorcerer and seer, the frenzied prophet, the man of destiny" (*Three Masters*, 142). This view of Dostoevsky as a prophet from the East was widely held in Germany at the time. In an essay written after the First World War and the Russian Revolution and entitled "*The Brothers Karamazov* or The Downfall of Europe" (1920), Hermann Hesse labeled Dostoevsky not a "poet" but a "prophet," a "sick man," with an "occult, godlike faculty" (119). He found in *The Brothers Karamazov* forewarnings of the coming downfall of staid Europe. The Karamazov family embodied the "Russian man," a being that combined "Good and Evil, God and Satan," and that would eventually overwhelm Europe. This "downfall," Hesse wrote, is "a return home to the mother, a turning back to Asia" and it will lead "like every death on earth, to a new birth" ("Downfall,"110, 108).

Sigmund Freud too sought to comment on *The Brothers Karamazov*. In a well-known essay entitled "Dostoevsky and Parricide" (1928) Freud subjected Dostoevsky's life and art to psychoanalytic interpretation. In Freud's view, Dostoevsky's Oedipal desire for his father's death and his concomitant feelings of guilt over the apparent murder of his father led to his epilepsy, and in *The Brothers Karamazov*, with its treatment of parricide and shared guilt, Dostoevsky made a long-delayed confession of his own inner urges. Thomas Mann, writing in a preface to a collection of Dostoevsky's short fiction, pursued the psychological angle on Dostoevsky as he connected the psychological depths found in the writer's work with Dostoevsky's epilepsy, which in turn was connected with the "realm of the sexual" ("Dostoevsky," x). Mann confessed that he was filled with "awe" in the presence of the "genius of disease and the disease of genius" in whom "saint and criminal are one" ("Dostoevsky," viii). Mann linked Dostoevsky with Nietzsche as "brothers in spirit" sharing such traits as "excess" and "satanistic moralism" ("Dostoevsky," xii). For Mann, "the watchword" was "Dostoevsky in moderation" ("Dostoevsky," xx).

Critical study of Dostoevsky and *The Brothers Karamazov* in the United States only began in earnest after the Second World

War. The 1950s saw the publication of noteworthy essays by Eliseo Vivas, George Gibian, and especially Philip Rahv. In "The Legend of the Grand Inquisitor'" (1954), Rahv examines Ivan's tale in light of the evolution of Dostoevsky's ideas on socialism, freedom, and Christianity. Characterizing the Legend as "one of the most revolutionary and devastating critiques of power and authority ever produced," Rahv argues that Dostoevsky was a novelist of "tragic freedom" who perceived that "genuine freedom, being open to the choice between good and evil, is unthinkable without suffering" (264, 270). In 1957, Ralph Matlaw's slim monograph *"The Brothers Karamazov": Novelistic Technique* appeared. Matlaw touches lightly upon a wide range of topics, including literary allusion, myth and symbol, and the role of the narrator.

Modern scholarship

It was during the next decade that the firm foundations of modern Dostoevsky scholarship in the United States were established. Over the course of the 1960s several monographs on Dostoevsky and *The Brothers Karamazov* appeared. These included Edward Wasiolek's *Dostoevsky: The Major Fiction* (1964); Donald Fanger's comparative study, *Dostoevsky and Romantic Realism: A Study of Dostoevsky in Relation to Balzac, Dickens, and Gogol* (1965); Robert Louis Jackson's *Dostoevsky's Quest for Form: A Study of His Philosophy of Art* (1966), with its seminal discussion of *obraz* (image, form) and *bezobrazie* (ugliness); and Robert Belknap's *The Structure of* The Brothers Karamazov (1967), which investigated "inherent relationships," clusters of associations, and varieties of narration in the novel. Not only did these scholars offer insightful analyses of key aspects of Dostoevsky's work, they trained and inspired succeeding generations of Dostoevsky scholars as well. Belknap went on to publish *The Genesis of* The Brothers Karamazov: *The Aesthetics, Ideology, and Psychology of Making a Text* (1990), Wasiolek translated and edited *The Notebooks for* The Brothers Karamazov (1971), and Jackson published two collections of essays: *The Art of Dostoevsky: Deliriums and Nocturnes* (1981) and *Dialogues with Dostoevsky: The Overwhelming Questions* (1993).

In the 1970s and 1980s the range and depth of Dostoevsky studies steadily expanded. A. Boyce Gibson (*The Religion of Dostoevsky*,

1973), Sven Linnér (*Starets Zosima in* The Brothers Karamazov: *A Study in the Mimesis of Virtue*, 1975), and Stewart Sutherland (*Atheism and the Rejection of God: Contemporary Philosophy and* The Brothers Karamazov, 1977) delved into the religious dimensions of Dostoevsky's art. Michael Holquist (*Dostoevsky and the Novel*, 1977), Malcom V. Jones (*Dostoyevsky: The Novel of Discord*, 1976), and Gary Saul Morson (*The Boundaries of Genre: Dostoevsky's* Diary of a Writer *and the Traditions of Literary Utopia*, 1981) explored issues of form and genre. Jacques Catteau published an illuminating examination of Dostoevsky's creative laboratory in *La creation littéraire chez Dostoïevski* (1978, translated and published in English in 1989 as *Dostoyevsky and the Process of Literary Creation*). Among other topics, Catteau discussed the role that Dostoevsky's concern with illness and money played in his creative process. James Rice also published an extensive study of the medical context for Dostoevsky's work entitled *Dostoevsky and the Healing Art: An Essay in Literary and Medical History* (1985), and Louis Breger studied the way in which psychological issues influenced Dostoevsky's work in *Dostoevsky: The Author as Psychoanalyst* (1989). Joseph Frank launched his exhaustive study of Dostoevsky's life and work in 1976 (*Dostoevsky: The Seeds of Revolt, 1821–1849*); the four remaining volumes came out over the next fifteen years (1983, 1986, 1995, and 2002); a one-volume condensed version appeared in 2010 (*Dostoevsky: A Writer in His Time*). Frank did a masterful job in detailing how Dostoevsky's works reflected and related to the events and ideas of their day. Finally, several studies devoted specifically to *The Brothers Karamazov* came out at this time. These include, in addition to Linnér's and Sutherland's monographs, Victor Terras's valuable *A Karamazov Companion: Commentary on the Genesis, Language, and Style of Dostoevsky's Novel* (1981), Nina Perlina's *Varieties of Poetic Utterance: Quotation in* The Brothers Karamazov (1985), and Valentina Vetlovskaia's *Poetika romana "Brat'ia Karamazovy"* (*The Poetics of the Novel "The Brothers Karamazov*," 1977).

Over the last two decades, scholarly study of Dostoevsky's works, and particularly *The Brothers Karamazov*, has grown exponentially. Robin Feuer Miller's The Brothers Karamazov: *Worlds of the Novel* (1992) provides a sensitive and insightful reading of the novel, while W. J. Leatherbarrow's *Fyodor*

Dostoyevsky: The Brothers Karamazov (1992) offers probing commentary on such topics as the family, the fragmented hero, and the ideas put forth by the Grand Inquistor. The religious and philosophical dimensions of Dostoevsky's art have continued to draw attention, and noteworthy contributions in this area are Liza Knapp's *The Annihilation of Inertia: Dostoevsky and Metaphysics* (1996), James Scanlan's *Dostoevsky the Thinker* (2002), Steven Cassedy's *Dostoevsky's Religion* (2005), Malcom Jones's *Dostoevsky and the Dynamics of Religious Experience* (2005), Rowan Williams's *Dostoevsky: Language, Faith and Fiction* (2008), Susan McReynolds's *Redemption and the Merchant God: Dostoevsky's Economy of Salvation and Antisemitism* (2008), and Diane Thompson's keen demonstration of close reading, The Brothers Karamazov *and the Poetics of Memory* (1991).

At the same time, the range of topics under consideration by Dostoevsky scholars has broadened significantly as well. Taking Dostoevsky scholarship in new directions or bringing fresh perceptions to old preconceptions are Harriet Murav's *Holy Foolishness: Dostoevsky's Novels and the Poetics of Cultural Critique* (1992); Nina Pelikan Straus' *Dostoevsky and the Woman Question: Rereadings at the End of the Century* (1994), an examination of Dostoevsky's handling of female characters from a feminist perspective; Deborah Martinsen's *Surprised by Shame: Dostoevsky's Liars and Narrative Exposure* (2003), a fascinating study of how Dostoevsky uses shame not only to expose his characters' psychology but to challenge the reader's response to events as well; Gary Rosenshield's *Western Law, Russian Justice: Dostoevsky, the Jury Trial, and the Law* (2005), an investigation of Dostoevsky's interest in legal issues and the way this is reflected in his writing; Susanne Fusso's *Discovering Sexuality in Dostoevsky* (2006), an analysis of Dostoevsky's treatment of adolescence and sexual awareness; Linda Ivanits's *Dostoevsky and the Russian People* (2008), which focuses on the role of folklore and folk belief in Dostoevsky's work; Ksana Blank's *Dostoevsky's Dialectics and the Problem of Sin* (2010), an examination of the pervasive role of contradiction and antinomy in Dostoevsky's fiction; and Carol Apollonio's *Dostoevsky's Secrets: Readings Against the Grain* (2009), an impressive re-evaluation of traditional conceptions about Dostoevsky's characters and the concept of virtue depicted in the fiction.

As noted above, *The Brothers Karamazov* has received its fair share of critical attention, and those scholars who have turned their focus onto the novel continue to find fresh topics and original perspectives. Representative of this trend is *A New Word on* The Brothers Karamazov, edited by Robert Louis Jackson. With over a dozen essays on a multitude of subjects, the collection lives up to its title by providing new evaluations of characters and themes, including revisionist appraisals of Smerdyakov (by Lee D. Johnson and Vladimir Golstein), an analysis of Zosima's confessional role (Caryl Emerson), and discussions of Grushenka's tale of the old woman and the onion (Gary Saul Morson and Kate Holland). Also worth noting is *Dostoevsky's* Brothers Karamazov: *Art, Creativity, and Spirituality*, edited by Predrag Cicovacki and Maria Granik (2010), which contains essays ranging from Ivan's devil to Islam. At the same time, new scholarship is proceeding apace in Western Europe and Russia too, and stimulating research has been produced by such scholars as Vladimir Zakharov, Tatyana Kasatkina, Igor Volgin, Lyudmila Saraskina, and Tatyana Buzina. The future for Dostoevsky and *Brothers Karamazov* studies is very bright indeed.

Notes

1 Analyzing Dostoevsky's work on the novel, Jacques Catteau has shown how ideas sparked by Dostoevsky's correspondence with his readers influenced specific incidents and phrasings in the work itself ("Whence Came Ivan Karamazov's Nightmare?," 65).

2 Review by I. Pavlov in *Rus'*, 29 November 1880 (cited in *PSS* 15: 499).

3 Review by V. F. Korsh in *Molva*, 19 October 1879 (cited in *PSS* 15: 491).

4 Review by L. Alekseev in *Russkoe Bogatstvo*, 1881, no. 11 (cited in *PSS* 15: 510).

5 Merezhkovskii, L. *Tolstoi i Dostoevskii: Zhizn' i tvorchestvo*, Part Two: *Tvorchestvo L. Tolstogo i Dostoevskogo*, 170 and 174. A partial translation of these essays can be found in *Tolstoi as Man and Artist with an Essay on Dostoevsky*.

6 For a detailed study of the Soviet reaction to Dostoevsky during

this period, see Vladimir Seduro, *Dostoyevski in Russian Literary Criticism 1846–1956*.

7 Cited by Mary Mackler in her introduction to Leonid Grossman's *Dostoevsky: His Life and Work*, xviii.

8 Ibid., xx.

9 Vladimir Seduro surveys the evolution of Dostoevsky criticism in the Soviet Union and in Russian émigré circles through the early 1970s in his *Dostoevski's Image in Russia Today*.

10 Murry would later recall that he was so captivated by Dostoevsky's work that he felt that he had become "hardly more than the amanuensis of a book that wrote itself" (*Autobiography*, 368).

11 For an analysis of Conrad's relationship to Dostoevsky, see Peter Kaye, *Dostoevsky and English Modernism*.

CHAPTER FIVE

Adaptation, interpretation, and influence

Theatrical and cinematic adaptations

Almost from the very moment of the publication of *The Brothers Karamazov*, attempts were made to stage theatrical versions of the novel. The imperial censorship office, however, blocked the earliest proposals to do so, writing in 1881: "The monstrous crime of parricide, in which three sons took a most active or unconscious part, cannot, in the opinion of the censor, be produced on the stage" (quoted in Ornatskaia and Stepanova, "Romany," 283). Four years later another proposal to mount a theatrical production met a similar fate: "This novel [...] cannot under any circumstances serve as a theme for reworking in a dramatic form for the Russian stage [...] realism is taken to extreme limits; transferred to the stage, this realism takes on the character of coarse and impudent cynicism [...] this work stands as a shameful stain on the Russian landowning class" (quoted in Ornatskaia and Stepanova, "Romany," 283–4).

At first, it was only possible for theatrical adaptations of the novel to be mounted in the provinces, away from the spotlight of Russia's main cities. In 1901, however, a production of *The*

Brothers Karamazov appeared in Alexey Suvorin's Maly Theater in St. Petersburg. Nearly a decade later, in October 1910, a major production of *The Brothers Karamazov* was put on at the famed Moscow Art Theater, under the direction of Vladimir Nemirovich-Danchenko. He decided to break the novel up into two sections that would be seen over two nights, and he attempted to focus the audience's attention on several intense scenes, such as Ivan Karamazov's encounter with his demon (staged by the actor playing Ivan alone, with only shifting shadows suggesting the presence of the mysterious interlocutor).[1] Although some reviewers criticized the performance, the show had many supporters, and it was Nemirovich-Danchenko's decision to follow up *The Brothers Karamazov* production with a new adaptation of Dostoevsky's *The Devils* that triggered Maxim Gorky's fierce rebuke to the production company. Nonetheless, the production enjoyed success both in Russia and abroad. Nemirovich-Danchenko himself declared that "Dostoevsky created a new epoch in the life of the Art Theater "(*Iz proshlogo*, 284). Over the decades since the first Moscow Art Theater production, stage adaptations of *The Brothers Karamazov* have been periodically mounted in Russia, with noteworthy productions occurring at the Moscow Dramatic Theater on Malaya Bronnaya in 1972 and at the Taganka Theater in 1998, under the direction of Yury Lyubimov.

Among the numerous adaptations of *The Brothers Karamazov* that have appeared in the West, an early French version done by Jacques Copeau and Jean Croué met critical acclaim upon its opening in 1911 at the Théâtre des Arts in Paris. Striving to fit Dostoevsky's copious fiction into five acts, Copeau and Croué created a highly condensed version in which the events of several scenes were compressed into a single scene, and numerous characters (the Snegiryov family, Kolya Krasotkin, Liza Khokhlakova, Ferapont) were entirely eliminated. The conclusion of the play focused not on Alyosha's speech to children, but on Ivan's mental and emotional collapse. The Copeau and Croué adaptation was translated into several languages, and stage performances followed in Belgrade (1913), New York (1914 and 1927), and Bucharest (1925).

In recent years, stage adaptations of *The Brothers Karamazov* have become even more popular, with a version by Anthony Clarvoe worthy of special note. Originally commissioned for the 1995 season of the Cincinnati Playhouse in the Park and the

Repertory Theater of St. Louis, Clarvoe's adaptation is swift-moving, highly condensed, and sometimes jarring in its language (Rakitin exclaims at one point: "Raise the skull and crossbones, boys, we're buccaneers now!" [49]). In it, Clarvoe touches upon the essential ideological and psychological concerns swirling around the Karamazov family (while leaving out Ilyusha Snegiryov, Kolya Krasotkin, and Liza Khokhlakova). The piece was directed by John Langs at the Circle X Theater in Los Angeles in 2005–6 and won five Garland Awards. Also distinctive is a fifty-minute piece entitled *The Grand Inquisitor*, which is an adaptation originally prepared by Marie-Hélène Estienne for the Théâtre des Bouffes du Nord in Paris, under the direction by Peter Brooks. The English-language version, performed by Bruce Myers, attracted great attention when it was put on at the Barbican in London in 2006, at the University of Maryland and the New York Theater Workshop in 2008, and at the Paramount Black Box Theater in Boston and the Broad Stage in Santa Monica, California in 2011.

Two operas have been based on *The Brothers Karamazov*, one by the Czech composer Otakar Jermiáš (1928), and one by the Russian composer Alexander Smelkov that had its premiere at the Mariinsky Theater in St. Petersburg in July 2008. The novel was also transformed into a two-act ballet in 1995 by Boris Eifman. In the ballet, movements of the body primarily do the work of Dostoevsky's words, and Eifman creatively handles such scenes as the conversation between the Grand Inquisitor and Christ by giving those parts to the dancers who play Ivan and Alyosha. The adaptations of the novel that have had the broadest impact, however, are the cinematic versions. The first film version of *The Brothers Karamazov* was a German silent film entitled *Die Brüder Karamasoff* (1921), directed by Carl Froelich and Dmitri Buchowetzki; Emil Jannings played the role of Dmitry Karamazov and Fritz Kortner played Fyodor Karamazov. Kortner came back to play Dmitry in a new version of the work entitled *Der Mörder Dimitri Karamasoff* (1931), directed by Erich Engels and Fyodor Otsep. An Italian rendition of the novel entitled *I fratelli Karamazoff*, directed by Giacomo Gentilomo was released in 1947.

In 1958, a major American production hit the screen. Directed by Richard Brooks and starring Lee J. Cobb as Fyodor, Yul Brynner as Dmitry, Richard Basehart as Ivan, and a young William Shatner as Alyosha, *The Brothers Karamazov* also featured Claire Bloom as Katerina and Maria Schell as Grushenka. Faced with the task of whittling Dostoevsky's expansive conception into a 150-minute package that would presumably appeal to an American audience, Brooks and company eliminated a whole series of characters and episodes that play important roles in the original novel. Gone are Kolya Krasotkin and Liza Khokhlakova, as well as Ivan's conversation with his devil. Most striking is the elimination of the spiritual conflict between Ivan's intellectual worldview and Zosima's doctrine of faith. Thus, the meeting between Ivan and Alyosha in which Ivan speaks of the suffering of children and narrates his tale of the Grand Inquisitor is eliminated, as is the biography of Father Zosima and the teachings he offers before his death. Nor does Alyosha undergo a crisis of doubt, be moved by Grushenka, or experience an epiphanic dream. In place of these elements, Brooks focused on the romantic intrigue involving Dmitry, Grushenka, Katerina, and Fyodor. He played up the atmospheric elements that an American audience might associate with Russia, including lots of gypsy music, balalaikas, dancing bears, and an improbable demonstration of horsemanship by Dmitry. The ending of the film ties up most of Dostoevsky's loose endings and puts a positive spin on events. Although Dmitry is convicted of his father's murder, he and Grushenka accept the escape plan hatched by Ivan. Ivan renounces his godless theories and embraces Dmitry. Dmitry goes to beg Snegiryov's forgiveness for insulting him in the marketplace, and little Ilyusha, rather than dying, allows his father to forgive Dmitry. While some of the actors manage to put up creditable performances, Lee J. Cobb is particularly effective, and he was subsequently nominated for an Academy Award for Best Supporting Actor.

The Soviet film studio Mosfilm released a new adaptation of *The Brothers Karamazov* in 1969. At nearly four hours in length, this version, directed by Ivan Pyryev in collaboration with Kirill Lavrov and Mikhail Ulyanov, was able to present more of the novel than the American version, but one notes the absence of significant elements, including the entire Ilyusha Snegiryov subplot as well as the characters of Liza Khokhlakova and Kolya Krasotkin. Father Zosima is given somewhat more attention, but his biography and exhortations are not included. Similarly, the filmmakers accorded Ivan Karamazov's spiritual dilemma more scope than the American version, but after Ivan (played by Kirill

Lavrov) offers a condensed version of his protest against the divine order and the suffering of innocent children, he makes no mention of the Grand Inquisitor. His later meeting with his devil is skillfully handled. Lavrov plays both Ivan and the devil, and as the scene progresses the devil's appearance becomes increasingly similar to Ivan's, thus emphasizing the notion that in talking with the devil, Ivan is talking with himself. After Zosima's death, Alyosha's moment of doubt is briefly presented, but he does not go on to have an epiphanic dream, nor does he make a speech about resurrection at the end of the film. Although Alyosha's faith emerges clearly in the work, the Soviet filmmakers presumably felt it prudent not to highlight Dostoevsky's ardent endorsement of Christianity as the solution to human problems. The film ends with Dmitry marching off to Siberia in a company of convicts, with Grushenka loyally following in a sledge through falling snow. The film consists of three parts, and the viewer observes a palpable shift in cinematic style after the first part. While many of the shots in the first part feature a fixed camera and one has the impression that one is watching a stage performance, in the second and third parts the camera is much more mobile, and there are more exterior scenes. Pyryev died during the filming of the piece, and the actors Lavrov and Ulyanov (who plays Dmitry) finished the film. The film was nominated for an Academy Award as Best Foreign Language Film in 1970.

The Brothers Karamazov has also been produced as a miniseries. An Italian version entitled I fratelli Karamazov was broadcast in seven parts in 1969, and a Russian production directed by Yury Moroz came out in two versions in 2009, an eight-part version for television, and a longer, twelve-part version released on DVD. Although Moroz introduced several alterations, cuts, and shifts in chronology (which results in the loss of some of the novel's subtlety and richness), his long version provides the most detailed and comprehensive treatment of the novel, and it does so with eye-catching scenery. Among the striking changes incorporated into the serial version, one can point to Dmitry's vision of himself being placed on a cross in his dream of the crying babe, and an eyewitness presentation of Smerdyakov's suicide. Then too, Moroz chose to end the work not with Alyosha's speech to the children after Ilyusha's funeral, but with a scene of Dmitry being marched off to Siberia under the gaze of Alyosha, Grushenka, Ivan, and

Katerina. This scene serves as the opening sequence for the titles in all the episodes.

The Brothers Karamazov has undergone other creative treatments as well, including a 1991 Russian film focusing on Kolya Krasotkin and Ilyusha Snegirov and the events of Book Ten of the *The Brothers Karamazov*. The film's title— *Mal'chiki*—is the same as the title of that book ("Boys"). In 2008, a Czech film based on the novel appeared. Entitled *Karamazovi* and directed by Petr Zelenka, the film features the preparations for a stage adaptation of Dostoevsky's novel to be mounted in a steel factory in Poland, and it deals with the connections between the themes of the novel and the lives of the people preparing to put on the production.

Literary influence

The influence of Dostoevsky's work as a whole (including such novels as *The Double, Notes from the Underground, Crime and Punishment, The Brothers Karamazov*) on world literature has been enormous. As the critic George Steiner put it in a comparative study of Dostoevsky and Tolstoy: "Dostoevsky has penetrated more deeply than Tolstoy into the fabric of contemporary thought. He is one of the principal masters of modern sensibility. The Dostoevskian strain is pervasive in the psychology of modern fiction, in the metaphysics of absurdity and tragic freedom which emerged from the Second World War, and in speculative theology" (*Tolstoy or Dostoevsky*, 346–7). Dostoevsky's depiction of a world wracked with doubt, his relentless investigation into the meaning and value of life, his questioning of traditional authority, and his search for something transcendent—all this has triggered a response from numerous writers. *The Brothers Karamazov* has been widely translated, appearing in the major languages of Western Europe as early as 1884 in German and 1888 in French.

The impact of *The Brothers Karamazov* can be detected in literature around the world. To begin with Dostoevsky's home country, one can find resonances of Dostoevsky's work in the creations of such writers as Vsevolod Garshin, Anton Chekhov, Ivan Bunin, Andrey Bely, Leonid Leonov, and many others. One of the most striking reworkings of ideas found in *The Brothers Karamazov* appears in *We*, a dystopian novel written by Yevgeny

Zamyatin in 1920. The novel depicts a rigidly ordered society devoted to principles of logic, reason, and science, and threatened by a group of freedom-seeking individuals encouraging rebellion and anarchy. The work displays strong links to Dostoevsky's *Notes from the Underground*, with its use of mathematical imagery as a marker of non-freedom, and in the stated goals of the so-called "Single" or "One" State, one recognizes a reformulation of the Grand Inquisitor's views on the necessity to deprive people of the burden of free choice, ostensibly in order to give them happiness. On the very first page of the novel, its narrator, the builder of a spaceship called the *Integral*, copies out a proclamation from the newspaper about the mission of this spaceship: "You will subjugate the unknown beings on other planets, who may still be living in the primitive condition of freedom, to the beneficent yoke of reason. If they fail to understand that we bring them mathematically infallible happiness, it will be our duty to compel them to be happy" (*We*, 1). Later in the novel, one of the narrator's friends describes a piece he's composing in honor of the *Integral*, and he refers to the "ancient legend about paradise": "Those two, in paradise, were given a choice: happiness without freedom, or freedom without happiness [...] Those idiots chose freedom, and what came of it? Of course, for ages afterward they longed for the chains" (*We*, 61). In these words one hears an echo of the Grand Inquisitor's claim that in the end, people "will lay their freedom at our feet" (220; see also 224, 225).

The clearest expression of the connections between Zamyatin's and Dostoevsky's novel comes in the figure of the "Benefactor," the ruler of this state whom the narrator characterizes as "as wise and loving-cruel as the Jehovah of the ancients" (*We*, 140–1). Like the Grand Inquisitor, this Benefactor presents himself as laboring under a burden of painful self-sacrifice. Evoking the scene of Christ's crucifixion, the Benefactor asks: "Does it not seem to you that the role of those above is the most difficult, the most important?" (*We*, 213). Once again, he articulates the essential trade-off that he and the other wise rulers have arranged for the masses: "what did people—from their very infancy—pray for, dream about, long for? They longed for someone to tell them, once and for all, the meaning of happiness, and then to bind them to it with a chain" (*We*, 214). The narrator finally succumbs to this logic and undergoes an operation to remove his imagination, but as the novel ends, the rebellion continues, and the outcome is uncertain.

The dystopian strain that Zamyatin detected in the Grand Inquisitor's vision of achieving human happiness by taking away human freedom piqued the interests of English writers as well. Like *We*, Aldous Huxley's *Brave New World* (1932) focuses on a world in which society has been organized in such a way as to ensure people's happiness through control over nearly every aspect of their lives, including work, play, and sexual gratification. Like *We* and *The Brothers Karamazov*, Huxley's novel features a powerful ruler figure who discusses the price that must be paid for human happiness and the personal cost that must be borne by the rulers who organize this system. Dividing people in a manner reminiscent of the Grand Inquisitor, the "World Controller" states that the optimum population is reminiscent of an iceberg: "eight-ninths below the water line" (these are the workers) and "one-ninth above" (these are the higher-functioning classes) (*Brave New World*, 268). Declaring that "the world's stable now" and that "[p]eople are happy," the Controller claims that he's had to sacrifice his own happiness for that of others: "That's how I paid. By choosing to serve happiness. Other people's—not mine" (*Brave New World*, 263, 274). Unlike *We*, however, the main rebel figure in *Brave New World* does not succumb to an operation that would reconcile him to this regime; rather, he commits suicide, and the novel ends with an image of his feet swinging freely under his hanging body. Huxley would go on to write a later essay entitled *Brave New World Revisited* (1958), in which he quotes several lines from Dostoevsky's Grand Inquisitor as he warns about the dangers of the loss of freedom in modern society.

The pessimistic ending of *Brave New World* may reflect the sobering conditions of the world in the first half of the twentieth century, and this mood of stark pessimism only grows thicker in the other major mid-century English-language novel that reflects the dystopian Grand Inquisitor vision, George Orwell's *1984*, published in 1949. Orwell's novel again depicts a society in which people have had their freedom taken away, but unlike *We* and *Brave New World*, this society is marked by ever-worsening deprivations and shortages. When Winston Smith, the rebel figure in the novel, is captured and brought to face O'Brien, a powerful member of the Inner Party, he expects O'Brien to try to justify the harshness of the system on the grounds that it is being carried out for the sake of the people's wellbeing: "He knew in advance what O'Brien would say: that the Party did not seek power for its own ends, but only for the good of the majority." In words that recall the arguments of the Grand Inquisitor, Smith continues imagining how O'Brien would respond: "That it sought power because men in the mass were frail, cowardly creatures who could not endure liberty or face the truth, and must be ruled over and systematically deceived by others who were stronger then themselves. That the choice for mankind lay between freedom and happiness, and that, for the great bulk of mankind, happiness was better." And again, echoing the notion that men such as the Grand Inquisitor suffer because of the deception they perpetrate on the people, Smith foresees O'Brien's subsequent argument: "That the Party was the eternal guradian of the weak, a dedicated sect doing evil that good might come, sacrificing its own happiness to that of others" (*1984*, 216).

As it turns out, however, Smith is mistaken, and the truth of the matter is more cynical and ruthless than he could anticipate. O'Brien declares: "The Party seek power entirely for its own sake. We are not interested in the good of others; we are interested solely in power." Speaking of past rulers, he says: "All the others, even those who resembled ourselves, were cowards and hypocrites [...] Power is not a means; it is an end" (*1984*, 217). With this assertion, O'Brien moves far beyond the Grand Inquisitor's supposedly selfless concern for the welfare of the masses and acknowledges that the enjoyment of power is itself the ultimate goal. Perhaps Orwell saw in the Grand Inquisitor's articulations of personal suffering an expression of that hypocrisy of which O'Brien speaks, and one recalls that Ivan's personal devil seemed to find in Ivan's schemes something less noble than what appeared on the surface. Referring to Ivan's concept of the man-God who has the ability to "lightheartedly overstep all the barriers of the old morality," the devil stated: "That's all very charming; but if you want to swindle why do you want a moral sanction for doing it?" (546). O'Brien frankly refuses to cobble together a "moral sanction" for the "swindle" he and the other Party bosses are engaged in. In this, perhaps, O'Brien sounds more like the character of Pyotr Verkhovensky from Dostoevsky's novel *The Devils* who ecstatically proclaims his goal of creating a society where he and a few others achieve absolute power over the masses who will be reduced to slavery. What is more, unlike the techniques for engineering human happiness employed by the rulers in *We* or *Brave New World* (sanctioning sexual promiscuity and idle amusements), which may stem from the Grand Inquisitor's vision of making the people's leisure time "like a child's game, with children's songs and innocent dance" (225), the masters of this new *1984* society have a more ruthless agenda: "Power is inflicting pain and humiliation [...] It is the exact opposite of the stupid hedonistic Utopias that the old reformers imagined [...] In our world there will be no emotions except fear, rage, triumph, and self-abasement" (*1984*, 220).

Ivan Karamazov had told Alyosha a story about how an abandoned Swiss child had grown up unloved and abused, committed murder, and then was indoctrinated by Christian clergy to repent of his crime, seek grace, and go to his execution praising the Lord (207–8). O'Brien describes something similar when he outlines to Smith the goal of his Party regarding the thought criminal: "We convert him, we capture his inner mind, we reshape him [...] We make him one of ourselves before we kill him" (*1984*, 210). Indeed, O'Brien's succeeds in crushing Smith's spirit to the point where Smith too, now a broken man, can only feel love for the ubiquitous Big Brother.

While the dystopian themes found in the Grand Inquisitor section of *The Brothers Karamazov* interested these English authors, Dostoevsky's appeal in general was of course much broader. In German literature, the impact of Dostoevsky's writings is evident in the work of several authors, including Franz Werfel, Rainer Maria Rilke, Hermann Hesse, and Franz Kafka. Kafka's private library contained editions of *The Brothers Karamazov*, *Crime and Punishment*, and *The Gambler*. In 1913 Kafka wrote his fiancée that he considered four men his "blood relatives": "Grillparzer, Dostoevsky, Kleist and Flaubert."[2] Kafka seemed particularly drawn to Dostoevsky's explorations of guilt and justice. His novel *The Trial* (published 1925) features a man, Josef K., who is accused of a crime, but the reader never learns what the crime is, or whether K. actually committed a crime. Initially, K. seems to treat the situation lightly, and he addresses the arresting officials somewhat like Dmitry K. did when he learned that he had not killed Grigory as he had originally thought. Dmitry had declared then: "I am ready, and we will make an end of it in one moment; for, listen,

listen, gentlemen! Since I know I'm innocent, we can put an end to it in a minute. Can't we? Can't we?" (391). Kafka's K. cries out: "Come, gentlemen [...] In my opinion the best thing now would be to bother no more about the justice or injustice of your behavior and settle the matter amicably by shaking hands on it" (*Trial*, 19). As time goes on, however, K.'s mood darkens, and his concern with his case becomes all-consuming. At the end of the novel, he is killed, still without ever having been informed of the specific charges, though now he seems thoroughly resigned to his fate. Unlike *The Brothers Karamazov*, the apparent guilt felt by Kafka's protagonist does not present a path to potential redemption. Rather it results in passive resignation and hopelessness.

Thomas Mann was deeply impressed by *The Brothers Karamazov*, and he incorporated some significant elements from it in his novel *Doctor Faustus* (1947). The narrator of the novel, like the narrator of *The Brothers Karamazov*, relates events that occurred several years in the past. Writing against the backdrop of the Second World War, the narrator delves extensively into such issues as human freedom and the struggle of good and evil. He records the teachings of theologians who ponder God's gift of freedom of choice to humans and the inextricable potential for evil that that freedom of choice entails. He recounts a theologian's story about the Inquisition, in which a woman who had supposedly pledged her soul to the devil falls into the hands of the Inquisition and repents of her sin, and ends up going willingly to her execution, preferring the stake to the power of the devil. This story recalls Ivan's narrative about the Swiss "savage" who repented of his sin and died praising the Lord. The novel itself focuses on the life of the narrator's friend—a composer named Adrian Leverkühn—who himself was interested in the religious dimension of human existence and who set to music verses from Dante's *Purgatorio* dealing with the torments of those righteous souls who died before being baptized. In a statement that has affinities with the Grand Inquisitor's view of humanity, Leverkühn finds that freedom always has a potential for "dialectic reversal": "It very quickly recognizes itself in restraint, finds fulfillment in subordinating itself to law, rule, coercion, system—finds fulfillment in them, but that does not mean it ceases to be freedom." To this, the narrator replies that "in reality that is no longer freedom at all" (*Doctor Faustus*, 203).

The most telling link between *Doctor Faustus* and *The Brothers Karamazov* is a scene in which Leverkühn has a conversation with a devil. The narrator provides Leverkühn's written recollection of the conversation, but he expresses his doubt that Leverkühn would have truly believed that what he saw and heard was real "despite the cynicisms with which his conversational partner attempted to convince him of his objective presence." But, in a phrase that echoes Ivan Karamazov's dismay at the appearance and conduct of the devil who appeared to him, the narrator continues about Leverkühn's demon: "if he, the visitor, did not exist [...] it is gruesome to think that the cynicism, the mockery, and the humbug likewise comes from his own stricken soul" (*Doctor Faustus*, 237).

There are several points of contact between the scenes of Leverkühn's and Ivan's conversations with their devils. For one thing, Leverkühn's devil initially appears in a lowly, trivial form: "a stocking-knit shirt striped crosswise with sleeves too short [...] trousers that sit untowardly tight, and yellow, overworn shoes ne'er to be clean again" (*Doctor Faustus*, 240). Over the course of the conversation, however, the devil undergoes several changes in appearance, only to end up in his original form. Like Ivan, Leverkühn initially insists that the devil is a projection from his own mind: "You say only such things as are in me and come out of me, but not out of you" (*Doctor Faustus*, 241). Yet Leverkühn's demon has not appeared simply to mock Leverkühn's ideas or instill in him a seed of faith. Here he plays a more conventional role, offering Leverkühn a demonic bargain: twenty-four years of brilliant creativity in return for his soul. Leverkühn has contracted syphilis from a prostitute, and the "illumination" of which the devil speaks may be merely a symptom of this disease. Yet the devil claims that the prostitute was a demonic agent, and that therefore Leverkühn has been enmeshed in the snares of the devil for some time. Leverkühn asks the devil what would await him in the end, after death, and the devil paints a picture of eternal torments that surpasses even Zosima's evocation of the spiritual abyss of hell: "'here all things cease,' every mercy, every grace, every forbearance, every last trace of consideration for the beseeching, unbelieving objection [...] it lies apart from and outside of language" (*Doctor Faustus*, 260–1). As a final condition of the demonic contract, the devil forbids Leverkühn ever to love another human being, and the meeting comes to an end with the arrival of one of Leverkühn's acquaintances.

Leverkühn goes on to become a great, if not universally popular, composer, and he chooses subjects with dark themes: *Apocalipsis cum figuris* and, appropriately, *The Lamentation of Doctor Faustus*. The composition of the last piece gained special urgency because of the death of Leverkühn's beautiful five-year-old nephew, whom the narrator characterizes with such words as "cherub-like," "enchanting," "inexpressibly sweet and pure" (*Doctor Faustus*, 489, 484). The agonizing death of this child so distresses even the narrator that he, like Ivan, seems on the verge of rebellion: "ah, my God, why do I seek gentle words for the most inconceivable cruelty I have ever witnessed, that even today goads my heart to bitter complaint, indeed to revolt" (*Doctor Faustus*, 496). Though the official diagnosis for the illness is cerebrospinal meningitis, Leverkühn blames himself for the child's death, for he had dared to love another human being against the devil's dictates. Like Ivan, Leverkühn suffers from headaches, and near the end of the narrative he experiences a complete mental breakdown. Just before this occurs, he tells a group of horrified acquaintances that he had been "wed with Satan" and was "born for hell" (*Doctor Faustus*, 521, 523). His final composition is described by the narrator as a "dark tone poem" permitting "no consolation, reconciliation, transfiguration" (*Doctor Faustus*, 515). But, in a gesture that represents the slightest ray of something positive, the narrator speaks of detecting in the final notes the possibility of "hope beyond hopelessness, the transcendence of despair—not its betrayal, but the miracle that goes beyond faith" (*Doctor Faustus*, 515). This is surely the hope that Mann himself felt about Germany's destiny as it emerged from the devastation of the Second World War.

While French writers, especially the Existentialists, found in Dostoevsky's work sources of inspiration for their view on human nature and the individual's relationship to the cosmos (see, for example, Albert Camus's *The Rebel* [1951] and *The Myth of Sisyphus* [1942]), writers in America discovered other riches. Although Dostoevsky had many admirers among American authors, including Theodore Dreiser, Sherwood Anderson, F. Scott Fitzgerald, and Richard Wright, his work made an especially powerful impression on Southern writers. As Maria Bloshteyn has argued, Dostoevsky's metaphysical orientation, his depictions of the struggle between faith and doubt, his interest in suffering as a potential path to redemption, and his belief that Russia was a special land misunderstood and often denigrated by others, played a major role in the Southerners' appreciation of his work ("Dostoevsky and the Literature of the American South" 6–11). Then too, Dostoevsky's late work revealed his interest in the relationship between masters and servants during a time of social transformation, as well as his enduring fascination with the dynamics of unsettled families. Several Southern writers cited Dostoevsky's importance as a writer. Carson McCullers wrote that she first read Dostoevsky with a "shock" she would never forget. His works "opened the door to an immense and marvelous new world" ("Books I Remember," 122). Walker Percy placed Dostoevsky first in a list of writers who "meant the most" to him (Lawson, *Conversations*, 5), and he declared that *The Brothers Karamazov* was "maybe the greatest novel of all time" (Lawson, *More Conversations*, 224). William Faulkner acknowledged in 1957 that Dostoevsky "is one who has not only influenced me a lot, but that I have got a great deal of pleasure out of reading, and I still read him again every year or so" (Gwynn, *Faulkner in the University*, 69). As Arthur Kinney has pointed out, Faulkner owned three copies of *The Brothers Karamazov* when he died (*Faulkner's Narrative Poetics*, 51).

Not surprisingly, then, references to and echoes from Dostoevsky's last novel are evident in the work of these writers. Walker Percy, for example, recasts in his novel *The Moviegoer* (1961) the exhortations that Alyosha Karamazov made in his speech to the children after Ilyusha's death in the concluding scene of *The Brothers Karamazov*. A child, the half-brother of the narrator Binx, lies dying in a hospital, while outside, one of the other siblings asks Binx: "When Our Lord raises us up on the last day, will Lonnie still be in a wheelchair or will he be like us?" Binx answers: "He'll be like you." After Binx assures the children that Lonnie will even be able to ski, the children cry "Hurray!" (*Moviegoer*, 190). Percy himself asserted that the last two pages of *The Moviegoer* "were meant as a conscious salute to Dostoevsky, in particular to the last few pages of *The Brothers Karamazov*" (*Conversations*, 75). Thomas Wolfe also refers to this scene from *The Brothers Karamazov* in his novel *The Web and the Rock*, which was published after his death, in 1939. The protagonist,

George Webber, delivers a passionate defense of Dostoevsky's novel and he singles out Alyosha's speech to the boys as especially meritorious. After summarizing the speech, he declares: "And these simple words move us more than the most elaborate rhetoric could do, because suddenly we know that we have been told something true and everlasting about life, and that the man who told it to us was right" (*The Web and the Rock*, 213). Critics have also detected echoes of *The Brothers Karamazov* in Wolfe's most famous novel, *Look Homeward, Angel* (1929), which features a Southern family whose young sons strive to establish individual identities in the face of a powerful, and sometimes abusive, father.

Critics have identified Dostoevskian elements in William Faulkner's works as well.[3] To take just one text in which evident parallels to *The Brothers Karamazov* crop up, Faulkner in *The Wild Palms* [*If I Forget Thee, Jerusalem*] (1939) follows an ill-fated love affair between a young medical school graduate and a married woman who leaves her husband and children for her new lover. At one point, the young man soberly evaluates the coldness of the modern world in terms that remind one of Ivan's fantasy about the Grand Inquisitor: "we have got rid of love at last just as we have got rid of Christ [...] If Jesus returned today we would have to crucify him quick in our own defense, to justify and preserve the civilization we have worked and suffered and died shrieking and cursing in rage and impotence and terror for two thousand years to create and perfect in man's own image" (*Wild Palms*, 115) After his lover dies from the consequences of an abortion she had asked him to perform on her, he is arrested, and, facing a choice similar to that confronting Dmitry Karamazov after his arrest, the young man refuses the chance to escape that has been offered him by the dead woman's husband. Similarly, after he is convicted of manslaughter, he spurns the opportunity to commit suicide, preferring to suffer for his crime and to remain alive with his grief rather than choose what he sees as an easy way out.

Dostoevsky's appeal in the United States reached beyond the South, of course. Kurt Vonnegut, for one, put into the words of one of his characters in *Slaughterhouse Five* (1969) the memorable assertion: "everything there was to know about life was in *The Brothers Karamazov*, by Feodor Dostoevsky." "But," the character continues: "that isn't *enough* anymore" (*Slaughterhouse Five*, 129). Vonnegut's novel, however, exhibits only tenuous links with

Dostoevsky's work. Vonnegut shares Dostoevsky's concern with inexplicable and seemingly gratuitous suffering, and he subtitled his novel "The Children's Crusade." One character displays the vicious temperament of Smerdyakov, and he proudly relates how he got revenge on a dog that bit him by putting metal shards in a piece of steak and feeding it to the dog—a clear reminder of the nasty trick that Smerdyakov suggested to Ilyusha (putting a pin in a lump of bread and feeding it to a dog). Unlike in Dostoevsky's novel, however, the dog in Vonnegut's novel swallows the steak and tears his insides. Vonnegut's novel, indeed, lacks the religious fervor and faith of Dostoevsky's work; the most comforting message it can offer is for one to try to ignore the awful times and "concentrate on the good ones" (*Slaughterhouse Five*, 150).

Connections to *The Brothers Karamazov* are foregrounded more prominently in David James Duncan's novel *The Brothers K* (1992). A stirring saga about the lives of the Chance family in Washington State, the novel focuses on the growth and maturation of three brothers in a household dominated by a baseball pitching father and a devout Seventh-day Adventist mother. Primarily narrated by the fourth brother, the novel is studded with reminiscences from Dostoevsky's text. Quotations from Dostoevsky's characters appear at significant moments in Duncan's work, and one can draw broad parallels between his characters' personality orientations and those of Dostoevsky's Karamazov brothers: Everett shares Dmitry's impetuousness, and winds up serving a term of penal servitude; Peter is an intellectual avidly searching for meaning (and peace) in life; and Irwin clings to a deep faith that leads him into a serious conflict with the military authorities during the Vietnam War. There are also two sisters in the family, and one of them has tortured dreams that remind the reader of Liza Khokhlakova's dream. Duncan's appreciation for Dostoevsky extends beyond Dostoevsky's last novel, however. A child is named Myshkin, and Duncan's narrator jokingly attributes a line from Kenny Roger's song "The Gambler" to Dostoevsky's novel of that name.

A final work of recent American fiction attests to the enduring appeal of *The Brothers Karamazov* on a new generation of writers. In 2007, Dinaw Mengestu, an immigrant from Ethiopia, published his first novel, *The Beautiful Things that Heaven Bears*. The narrator of the novel bonds with a neighbor's young daughter by reading to her *The Brothers Karamazov* at her prompting. When her mother takes the daughter away, the narrator is left to finish the novel himself, and he recalls reading aloud to the empty shelves of his small urban store his favorite passage, Alyosha's speech to the boys about the importance of preserving a sacred memory from childhood. As works such as this demonstrate, Dostoevsky's fiction continues to touch the spirits of creative figures, and it seems likely to do so for years to come.

Notes

1   See Sergei Bertensson, "The *Brothers Karamazov* at the Moscow Art Theater."

2   Quoted by Roman S. Struc in his article "Kafka and Dostoevsky as 'Blood Relatives'" (112).

3   For a detailed examination of the relationship between Faulkner's work and Dostoevsky's work, see Jean Weisgerber's *Faulkner and Dostoevsky.*

GUIDE TO FURTHER READING

The Brothers Karamazov— Selected Bibliography with Additional Works Cited

Modern critical editions of *The Brothers Karamazov*

The Brothers Karamazov. Trans. Constance Garnett. Revised by Ralph E. Matlaw and Susan McReynolds Oddo. New York, NY: W. W. Norton, 2011.

The Brothers Karamazov. Trans. David McDuff. New York. Penguin, 1993.

The Brothers Karamazov. Trans. Richard Pevear and Larissa Volokhonsky. New York, NY: Farrar, Straus and Giroux, 2002.

The Karamazov Brothers. Trans. Ignat Avsey. New York, NY: Oxford University Press, 1994.

Other featured works by Dostoevsky

The Adoloscent. Trans. Andrew MacAndrew. Garden City, NY: Anchor Books, 1972.

Complete Letters. 5 vols. Trans. and (ed.) David Lowe. Ann Arbor, MI: Ardis, 1988–91.

The Notebooks for The Brothers Karamazov. Trans. and (ed.) Edward Wasiolek. Chicago, IL: University of Chicago Press, 1971.

Notes from the Underground. Trans. Mirra Ginsburg. New York, NY: Bantam, 1983.

Polnoe sobranie sochinenii v tridtsati tomakh. 30 vols. Leningrad: Nauka, 1972–1990.

A Writer's Diary. 2 vols. Trans. Kenneth Lantz. Evanston, IL: Northwestern University Press, 1993–4.

Monographs

Anderson, Roger B. *Dostoevsky: Myths of Duality*. Gainesville, FL: University of Florida Press, 1986.

Apollonio, Carol. *Dostoevsky's Secrets: Readings Against the Grain*. Evanston, IL: Northwestern University Press, 2009.

Bakhtin, Mikhail. *Problems of Dostoevsky's Poetics*. Trans. and (ed.) Caryl Emerson. Minneapolis, MN: University of Minnesota Press, 1987.

Banerjee, Maria Nemcová. *Dostoevsky and the Scandal of Reason*. Great Barrington, MA: Lindisfarne Books, 2006.

Belknap, Robert L. *The Genesis of* The Brothers Karamazov: *The Aesthetics, Ideology, and Psychology of Making a Text*. Evanston, IL: Northwestern University Press, 1990.

—*The Structure of* The Brothers Karamazov. 1967. Reprint, Evanston, IL: Northwestern University Press, 1989.

Berdyaev, Nicholas. *Dostoevsky*. Trans. Donald Attwater. 1934. Reprint, Cleveland, OH: Meridian Books, 1969.

Blank, Ksana. *Dostoevsky's Dialectics and the Problem of Sin*. Evanston, IL: Northwestern University Press, 2010.

Breger, Louis. *Dostoevsky: The Author as Psychoanalyst*. New York, NY: New York University Press, 1989.

Cassedy, Steven. *Dostoevsky's Religion*. Stanford, CA: Stanford University Press, 2005.

Catteau, Jacques. *Dostoevsky and the Process of Literary Creation*. Trans. Audrey Littlewood. 1989. Reprint, Cambridge: Cambridge University Press, 2005.

Cox, Gary. *Tyrant and Victim in Dostoevsky*. Columbus, OH: Slavica, 1984.

Cox, Roger L. *Between Earth and Heaven: Shakespeare, Dostoevsky, and the Meaning of Christian Tragedy*. New York, NY: Holt, Rinehart, and Winston, 1969.

De Jonge, Alex. *Dostoevsky and the Age of Intensity*. London: Secker and Warburg, 1975.

Frank, Joseph. *Dostoevsky: The Mantle of the Prophet, 1871–1881*. Princeton, NJ; Princeton University Press, 2002.
—*Dostoevsky: The Miraculous Years, 1865–1871*. Princeton, NJ; Princeton University Press, 1995.
—*Dostoevsky: The Seeds of Revolt, 1821–1849*. Princeton, NJ; Princeton University Press, 1976.
—*Dostoevsky: The Stir of Liberation, 1860–1865*. Princeton, NJ; Princeton University Press, 1986.
—*Dostoevsky: The Years of Ordeal, 1850–1859*. Princeton, NJ; Princeton University Press, 1983.
—*Dostoevsky: A Writer in His Time*. Princeton, NJ; Princeton University Press, 2010.
Fusso, Susanne. *Discovering Sexuality in Dostoevsky*. Evanston, IL : Northwestern University Press, 2006.
Gibson, A. Boyce. *The Religion of Dostoevsky*. London: SCM Press, 1973.
Gide, André. *Dostoevsky*. New York, NY: New Directions, 1961.
Grossman, Leonid. *Dostoevsky: His Life and Work*. Trans. Mary Mackler. Indianapolis/New York, NY: Bobbs Merrill, 1975.
Holquist, (James) Michael. *Dostoevsky and the Novel*. 1977. Reprint, Evanston, IL: Northwestern University Press, 1986.
Ivanov, Vyacheslav. *Freedom and the Tragic Life: A Study in Dostoevsky*. Trans. Norman Cameron. New York, NY: Noonday Press, 1971.
Ivanits, Linda. *Dostoevsky and the Russian People*. Cambridge: Cambridge University Press, 2005.
Jackson, Robert Louis. *The Art of Dostoevsky: Deliriums and Nocturnes*. Princeton, NJ; Princeton University Press, 1981.
—*Dialogues with Dostoevsky: The Overwhelming Questions*. Stanford, CA: Stanford University Press, 1993.
—*Dostoevsky's Quest for Form: A Study of His Philosophy of Art*. 2nd edn. Bloomington: Physsardt, 1978.
Jones, John. *Dostoevsky*. 1983. Reprint, Oxford: Oxford University Press, 1985.
Jones, Malcom V. *Dostoevsky and the Dynamics of Religious Experience*. London: Anthem Press, 2005.
—*Dostoyevsky after Bakhtin: Readings in Dostoyevsky's Fantastic Realism*. Cambridge: Cambridge University Press, 1990.
—*Dostoyevsky: The Novel of Discord*. New York, NY: Harper and Row, 1976.
Kjetsaa, Geir. *Dostoevsky and His New Testament*. Slavica Norvegica 3. Oslo: Solum Forlag / Atlantic Highlands, NJ: Humanities Press, 1984.
—*Fyodor Dostoevsky: A Writer's Life*. Trans. Siri Hustvedt and David McDuff. New York, NY: Viking, 1987.

Knapp, Liza. *The Annihilation of Inertia: Dostoevsky and Metaphysics.* Evanston, IL: Northwestern University Press, 1996.

Lantz, Kenneth A. *The Dostoevsky Encyclopedia.* Westport, CT: Greenwood Press, 2004.

Leatherbarrow, W. J. *A Devil's Vaudeville: The Demonic in Dostoevsky's Major Fiction.* Evanston, IL: Northwestern University Press, 2005.

—*Fedor Dostoevsky: A Reference Guide.* Boston, MA: G. K. Hall, 1990.

—*Fyodor Dostoyevsky: The Brothers Karamazov.* Cambridge: Cambridge University Press, 1992.

Linnér, Sven. *Starets Zosima in* The Brothers Karamazov: *A Study in the Mimesis of Virtue.* Stockholm: Almqvist and Wiksell International, 1975.

Lyngstad, Alexandra H. *Dostoevskij and Schiller.* The Hague: Mouton, 1975.

Maksimov, S. V. *Nechistaia, nevedomaia i krestnaia sila.* 1903. Reprint, St. Petersburg: "POLISET," 1994.

Martinsen, Deborah A. *Surprised By Shame: Dostoevsky's Liars and Narrative Exposure.* Columbus, OH: The Ohio State University Press, 2003.

Matlaw, Ralph E. The Brothers Karamazov: *Novelistic Technique.* The Hague: Mouton, 1957.

McReynolds, Susan. *Redemption and the Merchant God: Dostoevsky's Economy of Salvation and Antisemitism.* Evanston, IL: Northwestern University Press, 2008.

Meerson, Olga. *Dostoevsky's Taboos.* Dresden: Dresden University Press, 1998.

Mikhailovsky, Nikolai K. *A Cruel Talent.* Trans. Spencer V. Cadmus, Jr. Ann Arbor: Ardis, 1978.

Miller, Robin Feuer. The Brothers Karamazov: *Worlds of the Novel.* New York, NY: Twayne, 1992.

Mochulsky, Konstantin. *Dostoevsky: His Life and Work.* Trans. Michael A. Minihan. Princeton, NJ; Princeton University Press, 1971.

Morson, Gary Saul. *Narrative and Freedom: The Shadows of Time.* New Haven, CT: Yale, 1994.

Murav, Harriet. *Holy Foolishness: Dostoevsky's Novels and the Poetics of Cultural Critique.* Stanford, CA: Stanford University Press, 1992.

Panichas, George A. *The Burden of Vision: Dostoevsky's Spiritual Art.* Grand Rapids, MI: William B. Eerdmans Publishing Co., 1977.

Peace, Richard. *Dostoyevsky: An Examination of the Major Novels.* Cambridge: Cambridge University Press, 1971.

Perlina, Nina. *Varieties of Poetic Utterance: Quotation in* The Brothers Karamazov. Lanham, MD: University Press of America, 1985.

Rice, James L. *Dostoevsky and the Healing Art: An Essay in Literary and Medical History.* Ann Arbor, MI: Ardis, 1985.
Rosenshield, Gary. *Western Law, Russian Justice: Dostoevsky, The Jury Trial, and the Law.* Madison: University of Wisconsin Press, 2005.
Rozanov, Vasily. *Dostoevsky and the Legend of the Grand Inquisitor.* Trans. Spencer E. Roberts. Ithaca: Cornell University Press, 1972.
Sandoz, Ellis. *Political Apocalypse: A Study of Dostoevsky's Grand Inquisitor.* 2nd edn. Wilmington, DE: ISI Books, 2000.
Scanlan, James P. *Dostoevsky the Thinker.* Ithaca, NY: Cornell, 2002.
Steiner, George. *Tolstoy or Dostoevsky: An Essay in the Old Criticism.* New York, NY: Dutton, 1971.
Straus, Nina Pelikan. *Dostoevsky and the Woman Question: Rereadings at the End of the Century.* New York, NY: St. Martin's Press, 1994.
Sutherland, Stewart R. *Atheism and the Rejection of God: Contemporary Philosophy and* The Brothers Karamazov. Oxford: Basil Blackwell, 1977.
Terras, Victor. *A Karamazov Companion: Commentary on the Genesis, Language, and Style of Dostoevsky's Novel.* Madison, WI: University of Wisconsin Press, 1981.
Thompson, Diane Oenning. The Brothers Karamazov *and The Poetics of Memory.* Cambridge: Cambridge University Press, 1991.
Vetlovskaia, V. E. *Poetika romana "Brat'ia Karamazovy."* Leningrad: Nauka, 1977.
Wasiolek, Edward. *Dostoevsky: The Major Fiction.* Cambridge, MA: The M.I.T. Press, 1964.
Williams, Rowan. *Dostoevsky: Language, Faith and Fiction.* Waco, TX: Baylor University Press, 2008.
Ziolkowski, Margaret. *Hagiography and Modern Russian Literature.* Princeton, NJ; Princeton University Press, 1988.

Collections of essays

Apollonio, Carol, (ed.), *The New Russian Dostoevsky: Readings for the Twenty-First Century.* Bloomington, IN: Slavica, 2010.
Barnhart, Joe E., (ed.), *Dostoevsky's Polyphonic Talent.* Lanham, MD: University Press of America, 2005.
Bloom, Harold, (ed.), *Fyodor Dostoevsky's* The Brothers Karamazov. New York, NY: Chelsea House, 1988.
Cicovacki, Predrag, and Maria Granik, (eds) *Dostoevsky's* Brothers Karamazov: *Art, Creativity, and Spirituality.* Heidelberg: Universitätsverlag Winter GmbH, 2010.

Gerigk, Horst-Jürgen, (ed.), *"Die Brüder Karamasow": Dostojewskijs letzter Roman in heutiger Sicht.* Dresden: Dresden University Press, 1997.

Jackson, Robert Louis, (ed.), *Dostoevsky: New Perspectives.* Englewood Cliffs, NJ: Prentice-Hall, 1984.

—*A New Word on* The Brothers Karamazov. Evanston, IL: Northwestern University Press, 2004.

Jones, Malcom V., and Garth M. Terry, (eds) *New Essays on Dostoyevsky.* Cambridge: Cambridge University Press, 1983.

Miller, Robin Feuer, (ed.), *Critical Essays on Dostoevsky.* Boston, MA: G. K. Hall, 1986.

Pattison, George, and Diane Oenning Thompson, (eds) *Dostoevsky and the Christian Tradition.* Cambridge: Cambridge University Press, 2001.

Wasiolek, Edward, (ed.), The Brothers Karamazov *and the Critics.* Belmont, CA: Wadsworth Publishing Co., 1967.

Wasserman, Jerry S., (ed.), *Fyodor Dostoevsky: The Grand Inquisitor.* Columbus, OH: Charles E. Merrill, 1970.

Wellek, René, (ed.), *Dostoevsky: A Collection of Critical Essays.* Englewood Cliffs, NJ: Prentice-Hall, 1962.

Young, Sarah, and Lesley Milne, (eds) *Dostoevsky on the Threshold of Other Worlds: Essays in Honour of Malcom V Jones.* Ilkeston: Bramcote Press, 2006.

Articles and book chapters

Amert, Susan. "The Reader's Responsibility in *The Brothers Karamazov*: Ophelia, Chermashnia, and the Palpable Obscure." In *Freedom and Responsibility in Russian Literature: Essays in Honor of Robert Louis Jackson.* Ed. Elizabeth Cheresh Allen and Gary Saul Morson. Evanston, IL: Northwestern University Press, 1995. 105–18.

Anderson, Roger B. "The Meaning of Carnival in *The Brothers Karamazov.*" *Slavic and East European Journal* 23.4 (1979): 458–78.

—"Mythical Implications of Father Zosima's Religious Teachings." *Slavic Review* 38.2 (1979): 272–89.

Barineau, R. Maurice. "The Triumph of Ethics over Doubt: Dostoevsky's *The Brothers Karamazov.*" *Christianity and Literature* 43.3–4 (1994): 375–92.

Belknap, Robert L. "Memory in *The Brothers Karamazov.*" In Jackson (ed.), *Dostoevsky: New Perspectives.* 227–42.

Berman, Anna A. "Siblings in *The Brothers Karamazov.*" *Russian Review* 68 (2009): 263–82.

Børtnes, Jostein. "The Function of Hagiography in Dostoevskij's
Novels." In Miller (ed.), *Critical Essays on Dostoevsky*. 188–93.
—"Polyphony in *The Brothers Karamazov*: Variations on a Theme."
Canadian-American Slavic Studies 17.3 (1983): 402–11.
Browning, Gary L. "Zosima's 'Secret of Renewal' in *The Brothers
Karamazov*." *Slavic and East European Journal* 33.4 (1989): 516–29.
Catteau, Jacques. "Whence Came Ivan Karamazov's Nightmare?
(Correspondence and Literary Creation)." In Young and Milne (eds),
Dostoevsky on the Threshold of Other Worlds. 64–71.
Connolly, Julian W. "Confession in *The Brothers Karamazov*." In
Cicovacki and Granik (eds), *Dostoevsky's* Brothers Karamazov: *Art,
Creativity, and Spirituality*." 13–28.
—"Conflict at the Crisis Point: *The Brothers Karamazov*. In Connolly,
*The Intimate Stranger: Meetings with the Devil in Nineteenth-
Century Russian Literature*. New York, NY: Peter Lang, 2001.
203–46.
—"Dostoevsky's Guide to Spiritual Epiphany in *The Brothers
Karamazov*." *Studies in East European Thought* 59 (2007): 39–54.
Contino, Paul J. "Incarnational Realism and the Case for Casuistry:
Dmitry Karamazov's Escape." In Cicovacki and Granik (eds),
Dostoevsky's Brothers Karamazov: *Art, Creativity, and Spirituality*."
131–58
—"Zosima, Mikhail and Prosaic Confessional Dialogue in Dostoevsky's
Brothers Karamazov," *Studies in the Novel* 27.1 (1995): 63–86.
Corrigan, Kevin. "Ivan's Devil in *The Brothers Karamazov* in the Light
of a Traditional Platonic View of Evil." *Forum for Modern Language
Studies* 22.1 (1986): 1–9.
Danow, David K. "Subtexts of *The Brothers Karamazov*." *Russian
Literature* 11 (1982): 173–208.
Emerson, Caryl. "Zosima's 'Mysterious Visitor': Again Bakhtin on
Dostoevsky, and Dostoevsky on Heaven and Hell." In Jackson (ed.),
New Word. 155–79.
Flath, Carol A. "The *Passion* of Dmitrii Karamazov." *Slavic Review* 58.3
(1999): 584–99.
Gibian, George. "Dostoevskij's Use of Russian Folklore." *Journal of
American Folklore* 69 (1956): 239–53.
Goldstein, Martin. "The Debate in *The Brothers Karamazov*." *Slavic and
East European Journal* 14.3 (1970): 326–40.
Golstein, Vladimir. "Accidental Families and Surrogate Fathers: Richard,
Grigory, and Smerdyakov." In Jackson (ed.), *New Word*, 90–106.
Hackel, Sergei. "The Religious Dimension: Vision or Evasion? Zosima's
Discourse in *The Brothers Karamazov*." In Jones and Terry (eds),
New Essays on Dostoyevsky. 139–68.

Holland, Kate. "Novelizing Religious Experience: The Generic Landscape of *The Brothers Karamazov*." *Slavic Review* 66.1 (2007): 63–81.

—"The Legend of the *Ladonka* and the Trial of the Novel." In Jackson (ed.), *New Word*. 192–99.

Hruska, Anne. "The Sins of Children in *The Brothers Karamazov*: Serfdom, Hierarachy, and Transcendence." *Christianity and Literature* 54.4 (2005): 471–95.

Ivanits, Linda J. "Folk Beliefs about the Unclean Force in *The Brothers Karamazov*." In *New Perspectives on Nineteenth-Century Russian Prose*. Ed. George J. Gutsche and Lauren G. Leighton. Columbus, OH: Slavica, 1982. 135–46.

—"Hagiography in *Brat'ja Karamazovy*: Zosima, Ferapont, and the Russian Monastic Saint." *Russian Language Journal* 117 (1980): 109–26.

Jackson, Robert Louis. "Alyosha's Speech at the Stone: 'The Whole Picture.'" In Jackson (ed.), *New Word*. 234–53.

— . "Dmitrij Karamazov and the 'Legend.'" *Slavic and East European Journal* 9.3 (1965): 257–67.

Johnson, Lee D. "Struggle for Theosis: Smerdyakov as Would-Be Saint." In Jackson (ed.), *New Word*, 74–89.

Jones, Malcolm V. "The Death and Resurrection of Orthodoxy in the Works of Dostoevsky." In *Cultural Discontinuity and Reconstruction: The Byzanto-Slav Heritage and the Creation of a Russian National Literature in the Nineteenth Century*. Ed. Jostein Børtnes and Ingunn Lunde (eds). Oslo: Solum forlag, 1997. 143–67.

—"'The Legend of the Grand Inquisitor': The Suppression of the Second Temptation and Dialogue with God." *Dostoevsky Studies* 7 (1986): 123–34.

—"Silence in *The Brothers Karamazov*." In Gerigk (ed.), *"Die Brüder Karamasow."* 29–45.

Kaladiouk, Anna Schur. "On 'Sticking to the Fact' and 'Understanding Nothing': Dostoevsky and the Scientific Method." *Russian Review* 65.3 (2006): 417–38.

Kallistos, Rt. Revd. [Timothy Ware]. "The Fool in Christ as Prophet and Apostle." *Sobornost* 6.2 (1984): 6–28.

Kanevskaia, Marina. "Smerdiakov and Ivan: Dostoevsky's *The Brothers Karamazov*." *Russian Review* 61.3 (2002): 358–76.

Kantor, Vladimir. "Pavel Smerdyakov and Ivan Karamazov: The Problem of Temptation." In Pattison and Thompson (eds), *Dostoevsky and the Christian Tradition*. 189–225.

Kanzer, Mark. "The Vision of Father Zossima from *The Brothers Karamazov*." *The American Imago* 8.4 (1951): 329–35.

Katz, Michael R. "The Theme of Maternity in Aleša Karamazov's

Four-Year-Old Memory," *Slavic and East European Journal* 34.4 (1990): 506–10.

Kelly, Aileen. "Dostoevskii and the Divided Conscience." *Slavic Review* 47.2 (1988): 239–60.

Kesich, Veselin. "Some Religious Aspects of Dostoyevsky's 'Brothers Karamazov.'" *St. Vladimir's Seminary Quarterly* 9.2 (1965): 83–99.

Knapp, Liza. "Mothers and Sons in *The Brothers Karamazov*: Our Ladies of Skotoprigonevsk." In Jackson (ed.), *A New Word on* The Brothers Karamazov, 31–52.

Meijer, J. M. "Situation Rhyme in a Novel of Dostoevskij." In *Dutch Contributions to the Fourth International Congress of Slavicists*. Mouton: The Hague, 1958. 115–28.

Miller, Robin Feuer. "The Metaphysical Novel and the Evocation of Anxiety: *Melmoth the Wanderer* and *The Brothers Karamazov*: A Case Study." In *Russianness: Studies on a Nation's Identity*. Robert L. Belknap (ed.). Ann Arbor, MI: Ardis, 1990. 94–112.

Morson, Gary Saul. "The God of Onions: *The Brothers Karamazov* and the Mythic Prosaic." In Jackson (ed.), *New Word*, 107–124.

—"Paradoxical Dostoevsky." *Slavic and East European Journal* 43.3 (1999): 471–94.

—"Verbal Pollution in *The Brothers Karamazov*." *PTL* 3 (1978): 223–33.

Moss, Kevin. "A Typology of Embedded Texts in *The Brothers Karamazov*." *Cornell Soviet Studies Reprint* 56 (1983).

Muchnic, Helen. "Ivan Karamazov: The Tragedy of Reason." *Zapiski russkoi akademicheskoi gruppy v SShA* 14 (1981): 138–57.

Murav, Harriet. "From *Skandalon* to Scandal: Ivan's Rebellion Reconsidered." *Slavic Review* 63.4 (2004): 756–70.

Natov, Nadine. "The Ethical and Structural Significance of the Three Temptations in *The Brothers Karamazov*." *Dostoevsky Studies* 8 (1987): 3–44.

Neuhäuser, Rudolf. "The Brothers Karamazov: A Contemporary Reading of Book VI, 'A Russian Monk.'" *Dostoevsky Studies* 7 (1986): 135–51.

Ollivier, Sophie. "L'Ambiguïté fantastique dans le chapitre des Frères Karamazov: 'Le Diable. Le cauchemar d'Ivan Fedorovič.'" *Dostoevsky Studies* 8 (1987): 121–33.

Rahv, Philip. "The Legend of the Grand Inquisitor." *Partisan Review* 21 (1954): 249–71.

Rosen, Nathan. "The Madness of Lise Khokhlakova in *The Brothers Karamazov*." *Dostoevsky Studies* 6 (2002): 154–62.

—"Style and Structure in *The Brothers Karamazov*." *Russian Literature Triquarterly* 1 (1971): 352–65.

Rosenshield, Gary. "Mystery and Commandment in *The Brothers Karamazov.*" *Journal of the American Academy of Religion* 62.2 (1994): 483–508.

Seeley, F. F. "Ivan Karamazov." In Jones and Terry (eds), *New Essays on Dostoyevsky.* 115–36.

Sewall, Richard B. "The Tragic World of the Karamazovs." In *Tragic Themes in Western Literature.* Cleanth Brooks (ed.) New Haven, CT: Yale University Press, 1955. 107–27.

Shrayer, Maxim D. "The Jewish Question and *The Brothers Karamazov.* In Jackson (ed.), *New Word.* 210–33.

Silbajoris, Rimvydas. "The Children in *The Brothers Karamazov.*" *Slavic and East European Journal* 7.1 (1963): 26–38.

Slochower, Harry. "The Pan-Slavic Image of the Earth Mother: *The Brothers Karamazov.*" *Mythopoesis: Mythic Patterns in the Literary Classics.* Detroit, MI: Wayne State University Press, 1970. 246–83.

Smyth, Sarah. "The 'Lukovka' Legend in 'The Brothers Karamazov.'" *Irish Slavonic Studies* 6 (1986): 41–51.

Stiver, Dan R. "Still Too High a Price? Ivan's Question in the Light of Contemporary Theodicy." In Barnhart (ed.), *Dostoevsky's Polyphonic Talent.* 25–39.

Surin, Kenneth. "The Critique of Traditional Theodicy: The Case of Ivan Karamazov." In Surin, *Theology and the Problem of Evil.* Oxford: Basil Blackwell, 1986. 96–105.

Terras, Victor. "On the Nature of Evil in *The Brothers Karamazov.*" In *Text and Context.* Peter Alberg Jensen et al. (eds) Stockholm: Almqvist and Wiksell, 1987. 58–64.

—"Turgenev and the Devil in *The Brothers Karamazov.*" *Canadian-American Slavic Studies* 6.2 (1972): 265–71.

Thompson, Diane Oenning. "Lise Khokhlakova: *shalunia / besenok.*" In *O Rus! Studia litteraria slavica in honorem Hugh McLean.* Simon Karlinsky et al. (eds) Berkeley: Berkeley Slavic Specialties, 1995. 281–97.

—"Motifs of Compassion in Dostoevskii's Novels." In *Cultural Discontinuity and Reconstruction: The Byzanto-Slav Heritage and the Creation of a Russian National Literature in the Nineteenth Century.* Ed. Jostein Børtnes and Ingunn Lunde. Oslo: Solum Forlag, 1997. 185–201.

Todd, William Mills III, "*The Brothers Karamazov* and the Poetics of Serial Publication," *Dostoevsky Studies* 7 (1986): 87–97.

—"Contexts of Criticism: Reviewing *The Brothers Karamazov* in 1879." In *Literature, Culture, and Society in the Modern Age. In Honor of Joseph Frank.* Part 1. Edward J. Brown et al. (eds) *Stanford Slavic Studies* 4.1 (1991). 293–310.

—"Serial Selves: Constructing Characters in *The Brothers Karamazov*."
In *Self and Story in Russian History*. Laura Engelstein and Stephanie
Sandler (eds). Ithaca: Cornell University Press, 2000. 266–79.

Vetlovskaia, Valentina E. "Alyosha Karamazov and the Hagiographic
Hero." In Jackson (ed.), *Dostoevsky: New Perspectives*. 206–26.

Vinokur, Val. "Facing the Devil in Dostoevsky's *The Brothers
Karamazov*." In *Word, Music, History: A Festschrift for Caryl
Emerson*. Part 2. Lazar Fleishman et al. (eds) *Stanford Slavic Studies*
29–30 (2005): 464–76.

Vladiv-Glover, Slobodanka. "Dostoyevsky, Freud and Parricide;
Deconstructive Notes on *The Brothers Karamazov*." *New Zealand
Slavonic Journal* (1993): 7–34.

Wasiolek, Edward. "*Aut Caesar, aut nihil*: A Study of Dostoevsky's
Moral Dialectic." *PMLA* 76.1 (1963): 89–97.

Wharton, Robert V. "Evil in an Earthly Paradise: Ivan Karamazov's
'Dialectic' against God and Zossima's 'Euclidean' Response." *The
Thomist* 41.4 (1977): 567–84.

—"Ivan Karamazov and the 'Crucible of Analysis.'" *Cithara* 28.1
(1988): 3–13.

—"Roads to Happiness in *The Brothers Karamazov*: Dostoevsky's
Defense of Christ." *Cithera* 23.2 (1984): 3–13.

—"Roads to Happiness in *The Brothers Karamazov*: Dostoevsky's
Defense of Christ: Part Two." *Cithera* 24.1 (1984): 59–70.

Whitcomb, Curt M. "The Temptation of Miracle in *Brat'ja
Karamazovy*." *Slavic and East European Journal* 36.2 (1992):
189–201.

Wood, Ralph C. "Dostoevsky on Evil as a Perversion of Personhood: A
Reading of Ivan Karamazov and the Grand Inquisitor." In Barnhart
(ed.), *Dostoevsky's Polyphonic Talent*. 1–24.

Journal

Dostoevsky Studies: The Journal of the International Dostoevsky Society.

Additional works cited

Contexts

Chernyshevsky, N. G. *Selected Philosophical Essays*. Moscow: Foreign
Languages Publishing House, 1953.

Dostoevskii, Andrei. *Vospominaniia Andreia Mikhailovicha
Dostoevskogo*. A. A. Dostoevskii (ed.). Leningrad: Izdatel'stvo
pisatelei, 1930.
Kostalevsky, Marina. *Dostoevsky and Soloviev: The Art of Integral
Vision*. New Haven: Yale University Press, 1997.
L'vov, F. N. "Zapiska o dele petrashevtsev." *Literaturnoe nasledstvo*.
Vol. 63. *Gertsen i Ogarev, III*. Moscow: Izd. Akademii nauk SSSR,
1956. 165–90.
Solovyov, V. S. *Enemies from the East?: V. S. Soloviev on Paganism,
Asian Civilizations, and Islam*. Trans. and (ed.) Vladimir Wozniuk.
Evanston, IL : Northwestern University Press, 2007.
—*Lectures on Godmanhood*. Trans. Peter Zouboff. San Rafael, CA:
Semantron, 2007.

Language, form, and style

Jung, Carl Gustav. *Two Essays on Analytical Psychology*. Princeton, NJ;
Princeton University Press, 1977.
Tolstoy, Leo. *Anna Karenina*. Trans. Louise and Aylmer Maude. George
Gibian (ed.). New York, NY: Norton, 1970.

Critical reception, composition, and publishing history

Baring, Maurice. *Landmarks in Russian Literature*. New York, NY:
Macmillan, 1912.
Bulgakov, S. N. "Ivan Karamazov kak filosofskii tip." *Izbrannye stat'i*. Vol. 2
of *Sochineniia v dvukh tomakh*. Moscow: Nauka, 1993. 15–45.
Camus, Albert. *The Rebel*. Trans. Anthony Bower. New York, NY:
Knopf, 1954.
Carr, Edward Hallett. *Dostoevsky (1821–1881): A New Biography*.
Boston and New York, NY: Houghton Mifflin, 1931.
Conrad, Joseph. *The Collected Letters of Joseph Conrad*. Vol. 6,
1917–1919. Cambridge: Cambridge University Press, 2002.
Freud, Sigmund. "Dostoevsky and Parricide." In Wellek (ed.),
Dostoevsky. 98–111.
Gor'kii, M. "O 'karamazovshchine.'" In *O literature*. Moscow: Gos. izd.
khudozhestvennoi literatury, 1961. 66–9.
Gorky, M. "Soviet Literature." In *On Literature*. Moscow: Foreign
Languages Publishing House, 1960. 228–68.

Hesse, Hermann. "The Downfall of Europe. 'The Brothers Karamazoff,'" *English Review* 35 (1922): 108–20.

Kaye, Peter. *Dostoevsky and English Modernism, 1900–1930.* Cambridge: Cambridge University Press, 1999.

Krinitsyn, A. B. "Dostoevskii v Germanii." In *Dostoevskii i XX vek.* Vol. 2. Ed. T. A. Kasatkina. Moscow: IMLI RAN, 2007. 178–249.

Lawrence, D. H. "Introduction." In Fyodor Dostoevsky, *The Grand Inquisitor*, trans. S. S. Koteliansky. London: Martin Secker, 1935. 5–23.

—*The Letters of D. H. Lawrence.* Ed. Aldous Huxley. New York, NY: Viking, 1932.

Leont'ev, Konstantin. "O vsemirnoi liubvi." In *Kriticheskie stat'i.* Vol. 8 of *Sobranie sochinenii.* Moscow: Izdanie V. M. Sablina, 1912. 175–212.

Lloyd, J. A. T. *Feodor Dostoieffsky: A Great Russian Realist.* New York, NY: John Lane, 1914.

Mann, Thomas. "Dostoevsky—in Moderation." In *The Short Novels of Dostoevsky.* New York, NY: Dial Press, 1945. vii–xx.

Merezhkovksii, Dmitrii. *L. Tolstoi i Dostoevskii: Zhizn' i tvorchestvo.* Part 2. *Tvorchestvo L. Tolstogo i Dostoevskogo.* Vol. 10 of *Polnoe sobranie sochinenii Dmitriia Sergeevicha Merezhkovskogo.* 1914. Reprint, Hildesheim, Georg Olms Verlag, 1973.

—*Tolstoi as Man and Artist with an Essay on Dostoïevski.* 1902. Reprint, Westport, CT: Greenwood Press, 1970.

Mirsky, D. S. "Preface." In *Dostoevsky (1821–1881): A New Biography* by Edward Hallett Carr. Boston, MA: Houghton Mifflin Co., 1931.

Murry, J. Middleton. *The Autobiography of John Middleton Murry: Between Two Worlds.* New York, NY: Julian Messner, 1936.

—*Fyodor Dostoevsky: A Critical Study.* London: Martin Secker, 1923.

Nietzsche, Friedrich. *Twilight of the Idols. The Anti-Christ.* Trans. R. J. Hollingdale. Harmondsworth: Penguin, 1968.

Seduro, Vladimir. *Dostoevski's Image in Russia Today.* Belmont, MA: Nordland, 1975.

—*Dostoyevski in Russian Literary Criticism 1846–1956.* New York, NY: Columbia University Press, 1957.

Woolf, Virginia. "The Russian Point of View." In *The Common Reader. First Series.* 1925. Reprint, London: The Hogarth Press, 1984. 173–82.

Vogüé, E. M. de. *The Russian Novel.* Trans. H. A. Sawyer. London: Chapman and Hall, 1913.

Zweig, Stefan. *Three Masters: Balzac, Dickens, Dostoeffsky.* Trans. Eden and Cedar Paul. New York, NY: Viking, 1930.

Adaptation, interpretation, and influence

Bertensson, Sergei. "The *Brothers Karamazov* at the Moscow Art Theater." *American Slavic and East European Review* 16.1 (1957): 74–78.

Bloshteyn, Maria. "Dostoevsky and the Literature of the American South." *Southern Literary Journal* 37.1 (2004): 1–24.

Clarvoe, Anthony. *The Brothers Karamazov: Based on the Novel by Fyodor Dostoevsky*. New York, NY: Broadway Play Publishing, 1997.

Copeau, Jacques, and Jean Croué. *The Brothers Karamazov: A Play in Five Acts*. 1927. Trans. Frank J. Morlock. Rockville: Borgo Press, 2011.

Faulkner, William. *The Wild Palms [If I Forget Thee, Jerusalem]*. New York, NY: Vintage, 1995.

Gwynn, Frederick L. and Joseph L. Blotner (eds). *Faulkner in the University*. New York, NY: Vintage, 1965.

Huxley, Aldous. *Brave New World*. New York, NY: Harper, 1946.

Kafka, Franz. *The Trial*. Trans. Willa and Edwin Muir. New York, NY: Vintage Books, 1969.

Kinney, Arthur F. *Faulkner's Narrative Poetics: Style as Vision*. Amherst, MA: University of Massachusetts Press, 1978.

Lawson, Lewis A. and Victor A. Kramer (eds). *Conversations with Walker Percy*. Jackson, MS: University Press of Mississippi, 1985.

—*More Conversations with Walker Percy*. Jackson, MS: University Press of Mississippi, 1993.

Mann, Thomas. *Doctor Faustus*. Trans. John E. Woods. New York, NY: Vintage International, 1999.

McCullers, Carson. "Books I Remember." *Harper's Bazaar* 75 (April 1941): 82, 122, 125

Nemirovich-Danchenko, Vladimir. *Iz proshlogo*. Moscow: Academia, 1936.

Ornatskaia, T. I. and G. V. Stepanova. "Romany Dostoevskogo i dramaticheskaia tsenzura." In *Dostoevskii: Materialy i issledovaniia*. Vol 1. Leningrad: Nauka, 1974. 268–85.

Orwell, George. *1984*. New York, NY: Signet, 1983.

Percy, Walker. *The Moviegoer*. New York, NY: Bard, 1982.

Struc, Roman S. "Kafka and Dostoevsky as 'Blood Relatives.'" *Dostoevsky Studies* 2 (1981): 111–17

Vonnegut, Kurt. *Slaughterhouse Five or The Children's Crusade: A Duty-Dance with Death*. New York, NY: Dial Press, 2009.

Weisgerber, Jean. *Faulkner and Dostoevsky: Influence and Confluence*. Trans. Dean McWiliams. Athens, OH: Ohio University Press, 1974.

Wolfe, Thomas. *The Web and the Rock*. New York, NY: Harper and Row, 1939.

Zamyatin, Yevgeny. *We*. Trans. Mirra Ginsburg. New York, NY: Avon, 1972.

INDEX

BM: FJ indigo
hvy bandana
striped ws
indigo ws

CB: moleskin shirt
chambray ws
tie
tie

EBT waistcoat

BB jeans

OOR jacket
shirt

WHM vest
RR vest
vest